SCHEHERAZADE'S LAST NIGHT AND OTHER PLAYS

Publications of the North American Jules Verne Society

The Palik Series (edited by Brian Taves)

The Marriage of a Marquis
Translated by Edward Baxter and Kieran M. O'Driscoll

Shipwrecked Family: Marooned with Uncle Robinson
Translated by Sidney Kravitz

Mr. Chimp & Other Plays
Translated by Frank Morlock

The Count of Chanteleine: A Tale of the French Revolution
Translated by Edward Baxter

Vice, Redemption, and the Distant Colony
Translated, with notes, by Kieran M. O'Driscoll

Around the World in 80 Days: The 1874 Play

Bandits & Rebels
Translated by Edward Baxter

Golden Danube
Translated, with notes, by Kieran M. O'Driscoll

A Priest in 1835
Translated, with notes, by Daniéle Chatelain and George Slusser

Castles of California
Translated, with notes, by Kieran M. O'Driscoll

Worlds Known and Unknown

Editorial Committee of the North American Jules Verne Society:
Brian Taves, Jean-Michel Margot, Terry Harpold

Scheherazade's Last Night and Other Plays

by Jules Verne

Translated, with an introduction
and notes, by

Peter Schulman

Edited by Brian Taves for the

North American Jules Verne Society

The Palik Series

BearManor Fiction
2017

Scheherazade's Last Night and Other Plays
by Jules Verne

© 2017 North American Jules Verne Society

All rights reserved.

For information, address:

BearManor Fiction
P. O. Box 71426
Albany, GA 31708

bearmanormedia.com

North American Jules Verne Society: najvs.org

Typesetting and layout by John Teehan

Published in the USA by BearManor Media

ISBN — 978-1-62933-197-3

Table of Contents

Introduction 1

An Excursion at Sea 21

"Les Gabiers: Chanson Maritime" (song) 93

The Thousand and Second Night 97

La Guimard 133
    Act I 134
    Act II 181

Illustrations 221

Acknowledgements 223

Contributors 225

The Palik Series 227

Previous Volumes in the Palik Series 229

The North American Jules Verne Society 237

Jules Verne, the youthful playwright.

Introduction

Pre-Hetzel Verne: Bohemian Paris

An Excursion at Sea, The Thousand and Second Night, La Guimard... For over a hundred and fifty years, these plays languished in Jules Verne's desk and then on the dusty shelves of the Nantes Municipal Library before Christian Robin was able to publish them in 2005, in honor of the centenary of Verne's death. That anniversary triggered a plethora of commemorations, new editions of Verne's works, events, and conferences, among many different activities and endeavors. Robin's remarkable collection included all of Verne's previously unpublished plays in a volume titled *Théâtre inédit*, issued by the Cherche-Midi press in Paris.¹ All in all, Robin collected and edited twenty-one plays that, for the most part, had never even been performed, let alone translated into English. Fortunately, the Palik Series, in addition to stories and novels, and the plays in this volume, has also published the original translation of the theatrical version of *Around the World in 80 Days* (very different from the novel of the same title), along with six more plays translated for the first time in the volumes *Mr. Chimp, and Other Plays* and *Castles of California*.²

---

1. Jules Verne, *Théâtre inédit*, édition dirigée par Christian Robin, Collection La Bibliothèque Verne (Paris: Le Cherche Midi, 2005).

2. Jules Verne and Adolphe D'Ennery, *Around the World in Eighty Days—The 1874 Play*, the original translation commissioned by the Kiralfy Brothers (Albany, GA: BearManor Fiction, 2013); Jules Verne, with Michel Carré, Charles Wallut and Victorien Sardou, *Mr. Chimp, and Other Plays*, translated by Frank

One could be tempted to assume, to paraphrase Fran Leibowitz, that there had to have been a reason why these plays hadn't seen the light of day for all these years, besides the fact that people forgot about them in order to concentrate on Verne's more famous and beloved novels. One might question the quality of plays left to wither away in obscurity for over a century were the author of those plays not Jules Verne—and more importantly—were these plays not, in actual fact, theatrical gems, filled with whimsy, charm and even pathos. *An Excursion at Sea* (*Une Promenade en mer*, completed in 1851), for example, which contains a delightful song, "The Song of the Topmen" ("Chanson des Gabiers"), originally part of a series of poems Verne wrote in his early twenties, could easily have been written by Gilbert and Sullivan as it depicts a comical sea outing involving swashbuckling French smugglers pitted against an aristocratic English family taking a pleasure cruise on their yacht. *An Excursion at Sea* is an excursion that is delightfully lightheaded but also touches upon important Vernian themes of class, British-French rivalry, nautical adventures and hidden and revealed love. These are all themes that are found in, for example, *Five Weeks in a Balloon* (*Cinq Semaines en ballon*, 1863), and would be developed further in many of Verne's novels such as *The Children of Captain Grant* (*Les Enfants du capitaine Grant*, 1868), *Mathias Sandorf* (1885), and of course *Around the World in Eighty Days* (*Le Tour du monde en quatre-vingts jours*, 1872). The smuggler's boat in *An Excursion at Sea*, in fact, is named *Passe-Partout*, which prefigures Phileas Fogg's beloved manservant, but also the young Verne's artistic and real desires to *passer-partout*, to go everywhere and to have no limits in terms of imagination, art or travel. Indeed, the unpublished plays unearthed by Robin cover a wide scope of themes and historical periods: the corrupt Borgias in his very first play, *Alexandre VI* (also titled *Cesar Borgia*) in 1847; the Guy Fawkes' Rebellion in *The Powder Conspiracy* (*La Conspiration des poudres*, 1848); *A Drama Under Louis*

Morlock (Albany, GA: BearManor Fiction, 2011), including *Mr. Chimpanzee*, *The Knights of the Daffodil*, *An Adoptive Son*, and *Eleven Days of Siege*; Jules Verne, *Castles of California: Two Plays by Jules Verne*, translated, with an introduction and notes, by Kieran O'Driscoll (Albany, GA: BearManor Fiction, 2017), including *The Castles of California* and *A Nephew from America*. The North American Jules Verne Society's first book was *Journey Through the Impossible* (Amherst, NY: Prometheus, 2003), a science fiction stage original written in collaboration with Adolphe D'Ennery, translated by Edward Baxter.

Passepartout in the novel *Le Tour du monde en quatre-vingts jours* (*Around the World in Eighty Days*, 1873).

Exterior of the Théâtre Lyrique in Verne's time.

XV (*Un Drame sous Louis XV*) and *Abd'Allah* (both 1849) delve into 18th-century French society; and *The Thousand and Second Night* (*La Mille et deuxième nuit*, 1850) harkens back to romantic orientalist visions of the Middle East so admired by 19th century artists and writers such as Flaubert and Delacroix among many others ever since Antoine

Interior of the Théâtre Lyrique.

Galland published his translations of the *Arabian Nights* into French in the early 1700s.

As Jean-Michel Margot points out in his article "Jules Verne, Playwright," after the success of *Five Weeks in a Balloon*, among the others that would usher in Verne's gigantically popular career as a novelist with his editor P-J. Hetzel, Verne "was almost better known during this period as a playwright than as a novelist."[3] His production of *Around the World in 80 Days* (*Le Tour du monde en 80 jours*), for example, which opened at the Théâtre de la Porte Saint-Martin in Paris had, as Margot points out, "a hugely successful run of 415 performances."[4]

When Verne was writing *An Excursion at Sea*, however, he was making very little money despite having great ambitions of joining the

---

3. Jean-Michel Margot, "Jules Verne Playwright," *Science Fiction Studies*, 32 (2005), 153. For a much expanded version of this essay see Margot's Introduction in the Palik Series volume, *Mr. Chimp, and Other Plays*.

   For more on the play of *Around the World in 80 Days*, see the Introduction by Philippe Burgaud with Jean-Michel Margot and Brian Taves in the Palik Series volume, *Around the World in Eighty Days—The 1874 Play*.

4. Margot, "Jules Verne Playwright," 153.

Aristide Hignard, courtesy Volker Dehs.

literary heavyweights of his time such as Victor Hugo and Alexandre Dumas, who were known as much for their plays as they were for their novels and poetry. When Verne accepted the job as secretary for Dumas' Théâtre Lyrique (which had previously been called the Théâtre Historique when Dumas first ran it), Verne was only making about 100 francs a month with the added lure by Jules Seveste, the theater's director, that the theatre might produce a few of his plays. The youthful Verne enjoyed a bachelor but artistically stimulating life in Paris, when he moved near the theater district on Bonne Nouvelle, one flight above his comrade from Nantes, the composer Aristide Hignard (1822-1898), with whom he would collaborate on four musical plays as well as some poems of Verne's which Hignard put to music.[5] It is undoubtedly true, as Margot has pointed out several times, that Verne's plays would have been much more successful and might have avoided oblivion if he had collaborated not with Hignard but with Jacques Offenbach, whose theater, the Bouffes Parisiennes, had produced *Mr. Chimpanzee* in 1855. However, the truth of the matter is that Verne and Hignard were friends, practically roommates, and immersed themselves in the artistic fervor that spending one's beginning years in Paris as an artist could ignite. Together, they lived through the political upheavals leading to Napoleon III's rise to power and the astounding theater scene that lit up the Parisian boulevards in the 19th century. As Gilles de Robien explains regarding Verne's loyalty to Hignard:

> Ballasted by his friend Aristide Hignard for ten years already, Jules had difficulty taking off. Perhaps he should reconsider a collaboration that is taking too much time to show its fruits? Yet, convinced as he was of the incomparable genius of his fellow Nantes native, loyal and opinionated as he is in all of his relationships, he cannot imagine working with another composer. Perhaps Aristide's talent is less important to him than his friendship. Jules needs to breathe fresh air, the carefree and independent winds that the composer brings to the table.[6]

---

5. Some of Hignard's melodies were released in 2005 on a CD celebrating his collaboration, entitled *Jules Verne: Mélodies inédites*, by the Académie de Bretagne et des Pays de Loire.

6. Gille de Robien, *Jules Verne: Le rêveur incompris* (Paris: Editions Michel Lafon,

One of the Hignard-Verne musical collaborations, from 1856; note the respective billing of their names.

2000), 85, my translation.

Together, they would travel to England, Scotland, and Scandinavia, all resulting in writings by Verne.[7] Hignard was even a witness at Verne's wedding, and the two collaborated on four plays: *The Thousand and Second Night* in 1850 which was never produced; *Blind Man's Bluff* (*Le Colin-Maillard*, 1852), which they did with Verne's friend and co-librettist Michel Carré, along with *The Companions of the Marjoram* (*Les Compagnons de la marjolaine*) in 1853 which had 24 performances at the Théâtre Lyrique; and *The Ardennes Inn* (*L'Auberge des Ardennes*) which was also performed at the Lyrique in 1860 in addition to *Mr. Chimpanzee*.[8] All of these plays provided for a valuable testing period and a development of the writer's craft both in terms of Verne the dramatist and future novelist.

Hignard, besides putting to music some of Verne's early poems, also produced his own works, such as an opera based on Shakespeare's *Hamlet* (1857-63) which won the prestigious Prix de l'Académie de Beaux Arts in 1868, and a type of sequel to Moliere's *Monsieur Pourceaugnac* called *The New Pourceaugnac* (*Le Nouveau Pourceaugnac*) in 1860. In Paris, Verne and Hignard would live out the quintessential *vie de Bohème* during which many young writers, artists and composers would drop by their place and discuss their work. At one point, while he was still at the Lyrique, Verne created a weekly dining club called The Eleven Bachelors *(Les Onze Sans Femme)* where they would compose raunchy songs and skits.

As William Butcher describes it: "By some trick of fate, all of Verne's misogynous companions, although mostly unknown then, would, a generation later, form a roll call of the good and great."[9] As for Hignard himself, sadly and despite winning his prize for *Hamlet*, he never achieved the attention that would allow him to have a happy career in Paris. Shy and humble, he was largely forgotten and died in

---

7. Verne's accounts of these trips with Hignard would only be published well after the author's death: *Voyage à Reculons en Angleterre et en Ecosse* (Paris: Cherche-Midi, 1989); "Joyeuses misères de trois voyageurs en Scandinavie," *Géo*, Special Issue, 2003. In *Voyage à Reculons en Angleterre et en Ecosse*, the character Jonathan Savournon represents Hignard.

8. *Les Compagnons de la marjolaine* was translated by Frank Morlock as *The Knights of the Daffodil* in the Palik Series volume *Mr. Chimp, and Other Plays*.

9. William Butcher, *Jules Verne: The Definitive Biography* (New York: Thunder's Mouth Press, 2006), 94-95.

Cover of an 1892 translation of the Verne-Hignard stage collaboration, *The Ardennes Inn*.

Vernon in the care of his wife.

As the newspaper *Le Monde Illustrée* wrote about Hignard's music to *Mr. Chimpanzee*, Hignard's melodies were pleasant enough but tilted towards the strange and inaccessible. "Mr. Hignard's melodies are easy enough and he certainly knows how to bring them out, to shine light on them with all the resources of his art; he has, moreover, a marked tendency towards originality, or rather, as we fear, as though he were taken by an all too slippery slope towards the abyss of the bizarre."[10]

An Excursion at Sea

At first glance, *An Excursion at Sea* might seem but a trifle of a piece, as it was written as a *vaudeville*, a light comedy. It is the story of an encounter between a yacht, the *Saint-Dunstan*, and a French smuggling vessel called the *Passe-Partout* which is looking to unload its merchandise onto the Isle of Wight. As the *Saint-Dunstan* is running out of supplies, its owner and captain, Lord Gray, decides to teach the smugglers a lesson by attacking it while the sea is calm and, while they are at it, taking the supplies for his family, guests and crew. Lady Gray, their daughter Anna, Lord Packet (an elderly man whom she is supposed to marry) and Lady Ossulton (Lady Gray's cousin) all stay aboard while the men go off in a skiff to attack the ship. Lord Packet gets sick and complains of it throughout the play. When the skiff returns, however, it has been taken over by the French who seize the *Saint-Dunstan* and hold on to Lord Gray and his officers as prisoners. Georges, a young man secretly in love with Anna and disguised and hired as a midshipman, tries to liberate the ship for Anna but is himself captured and sentenced to death by Antoine, the French captain, who uses the English skiffs to unload his merchandise in relative safety. When Anna and Georges admit their love for each other before he is about to die, Antoine allows her to marry him (through a seaman's clause stating that a woman can save a man from execution if she agrees to have him as a husband). Although her father was bitterly opposed to the union prior to this event, he acquiesces as the play ends happily, merrily and in song.

Throughout this little play, however, one can see many Vernian nautical motifs. In addition to Verne's novels which feature sea adventures, Verne himself enjoyed his own yachts in later years. Although the play is extremely light, it could easily have turned into a tragedy, as most

---

10. Cited by Robien, *op. cit.*, 85, from *Le Monde Illustrée*, February 17, 1858, my translation.

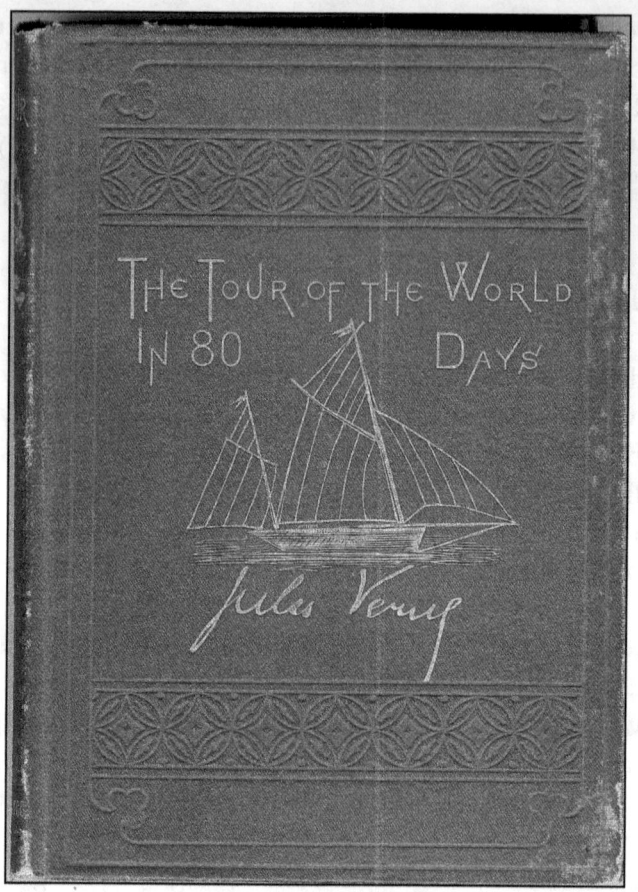

The Saunterer edition of *Around the World in Eighty Days*, published in the United States by Osgood in 1874, showed Verne's own sketch of his first yacht, *Saint-Michel*.

comedies could, under a different lens. Lady Ossulton fears cannibals for example and is hysterical over a potential shipwreck as she evokes the shipwreck of the *Medusa* immortalized by Gericault in his famous painting. Similarly, in *The Chancellor* (*Le Chancellor*, 1875), Verne writes harrowingly about the shipwreck of a British sailing vessel from the perspective of one of the passengers, in terms which Verne himself described as displaying "terrifying realism."[11] Yet, as it is a young man's comedy, *An Excursion at Sea* ends in marriage and with some bawdiness straight out of his bachelor club at that time. As Philippe Valetoux

---

11. Herbert R. Lottman, *Jules Verne: An Exploratory Biography* (New York: St. Martin's Press, 1996), 155.

Verne's third and final yacht, *Saint Michel III*, in 1886.

sees it, in his introduction, "the debauchery and vulgarity with its forced laughter nonetheless hides a romantic backbone to the story: the young midshipman is in love but, because of his social class, is prevented from marrying the one he loves."[12] For Philippe Valetoux, this predicament mirrors Verne himself at that time as he too was deeply in love with the beautiful but inaccessible Herminie Arnault-Grossetière, but couldn't marry her because he was not yet sufficiently established to do so.[13] She would end up marrying a much older man, similar to the play's Lord Packet, which was an event that broke Verne's heart and made him bitter towards such matches. Indeed, Verne had written over thirty poems to her and felt betrayed by her betrothal to a man with more money than him. As Verne wrote at the time, the pairing was one of "white hair mixed with black, the half-century married to the quarter-century."[14]

---

12. *Théâtre inédit, op. cit.,* 338, my translation.
13. Philippe Valetoux in Verne, *Théâtre inédit, op.cit.,* 356-357.
14. Lottman, *op. cit.,* 14-15.

Scheherazade: Verne-Poe-Gautier

When Verne wrote his comical *The Thousand and Second Night*, French readers had already been captivated by Galland's famous translation of the *Arabian Nights* from 1704 to 1719, but the idea of a thousand and *second* night was also conceived and attempted by Horace Walpole in his *Hieroglyphic Tales* (1766-1772) and then by Edgar Allan Poe and 19th century novelist Théophile Gautier who was known at that time for his fantastic tales. Poe's parody of the *Arabian Nights*, entitled "The Thousand and Second Tale of Scheherazade," was originally published in the Philadelphia magazine *Godey's Lady's Book* in 1845. In Poe's version, Scheherazade tries to stay alive by telling her husband a new story about Sinbad the Sailor, who goes to port one day seeking adventure and climbs onto what he thinks is a sea monster but is in reality a British steamship on which he is able to circumnavigate the globe (which he suddenly realizes is round and not flat), and discovers many wondrous things. Indeed, Poe's version is quite different from Verne's which he wrote as an exuberant operetta that ends joyously with the wedding of Scheherazade's sister Dinazarde to Hassan (which the Sultan opposed) and is interrupted by many duets and songs.

Yet, if Poe's version doesn't resemble Verne's, it *does* resemble—at least in the abstract—the concept of *Twenty Thousand Leagues under the Sea* (*Vingt Mille Lieues sous les mers*, 1870) in which the *Nautilus* is first taken for a giant Kraken before Aronnax and Ned Land realize that it is actually a submarine. They too, like Sinbad, will accidentally be able to go around the world (although underwater for the most part). While any comparison to Poe is merely speculative in terms of their writings, we do know that Verne greatly admired Poe and in fact wrote an article titled "Edgar Allan Poe and his Works" ("Edgar Poe et ses œuvres") for the magazine *Musée des Familles* (*Family Museum*) in April 1864, in addition to his amazing novel, *The Ice Sphinx* (*Le Sphinx des glaces*, 1897), which Verne wrote as a response to Poe's 1838 novel, *The Narrative of Arthur Gordon Pym*.[15]

Gautier's *The Thousand and Second Night* (*La Mille et Deuxième*

---

15. For more on Verne and Poe, see the critical material in the Palik Series volume, *A Priest in 1835*, translated, with an introductory essay and notes, by Danièle Chatelain and George Slusser (Albany, GA: BearManor Fiction, 2016).

Théophile Gautier

Nuit) is also completely different from Verne's as it is bracketed by a Parisian narrative which finds Scheherazade coming to Paris to ask a writer of serials to come up with a story for her as she has exhausted her supply. It was written in 1842, also for the *Musée des Familles* magazine, for which Verne wrote as well. Gautier's narrator provides the inspiration-drained Scheherazade with what would become Gautier's Oriental ballet, *La Péri* (1845), but it fails, nonetheless, to save Scheherazade's life as he learns that she was beheaded on returning home because the Sultan didn't appreciate the story. As the critic Dominique Julien has justly observed in her book on Scheherazade's reception in the 19th century, the *Arabian Nights* were pervasive within the French psyche.[16] In addition to Gautier's version, Scheherazade appears in Dumas's *The Count of Monte Cristo* (*Le Comte de Monte-Cristo*, 1845), and *The Mohicans of Paris* (*Les Mohicans de Paris*, 1854), and Eugène Sue's *The Mysteries of Paris* (*Les Mystères de Paris*, 1843), among many other works. In fact, as Edward Said has demonstrated so well in *Orientalism*, "orientalist" approaches to the Middle East were very much in vogue in art, music and literature in addition to being part of the European colonialist *zeitgeist*.[17] Of course, Verne's modest one-act cannot be considered a major part of the movement Said discusses, but it is a pleasant jewel of a play filled with comical scenes and charming songs. Once again, Verne ends his story with an optimistic wish fulfillment of love, rather than an unhappy ending such as Gautier's. As with Georges and Anna in *An Excursion at Sea*, Verne allows for an improbable wedding instead of an execution, as the Sultan who orchestrates it rediscovers his own love for Scheherazade and disavows his bloodthirsty pattern.

La Guimard: Artists, Muses and Artists

Finally, *La Guimard,* the longest play in this collection, was finished in 1853. It is inspired by the historical relationship between the famous dancer, Marie-Madeleine Guimard (known simply as "La Guimard," and who lived from 1743-1816) and the young painter Jacques-Louis David (1748-1825) before he became famous during the reign of Napoleon Bonaparte. La Guimard, in her heyday, was known not only for having been a brilliant ballet dancer at the Comédie Française but also for having been very *mondaine* and active socially. She had several powerful lovers and hosted stimulating parties. David had indeed made a portrait of her which she liked and as a result acted very generously towards him, as she protected him and supported his early work.

---

16. Dominique Julien, *Les Amoureux de Schehrazade: Variations modernes sur les Mille et une nuits* (Geneva: Droz, 2009).

17. Edward W. Said, *Orientalism* (New York: Vintage Books, 1979).

Frontispiece of *The Secret of Wilhelm Storitz*.

In Verne's version, however, la Guimard actively has a romantic relationship with David, and seduces him while he is in a relationship with a young woman named Valentine. In a Machiavellian spin on love, she will orchestrate Valentine's being placed in a nunnery to be married off by her guardian; David's winning the Rome Prize by setting up a jury that she can control; and eventually his liberation from the Bastille so that she can run off with him to Rome. When she sees that he and Valentine are really in love, she abandons her efforts and goes back to her art as she realizes that true lovers should be together. Although there are many comical moments in *La Guimard*, including some slapstick scenes with a couple of clumsy suitors, *La Guimard* is also a rather deep examination of love, art, the role of the muse in art, and the lives of painters. Moreover, La Guimard is not content merely being considered a muse, or an inspiration for great art; it is clear in Verne's play that she is the one who is very much in control and in the end, uses her power for self-sacrifice rather than selfish but fleeting pleasure.

Verne tackled a similar dialectic between a proto-famous artist and his muse in his one-act comedy *Monna Lisa* (*Mona Lisa*), which he worked and reworked on and off from 1851 to 1855.[18] *Mona Lisa* had only been permitted a reading in Amiens in 1874 before being published in French in the *Cahiers de l'Herne* in 1974.[19] In *Mona Lisa*, Verne focuses on a young Leonardo who is trying to capture the right smile for a portrait of Mona Lisa commissioned by her husband. Although Leonardo and Mona Lisa fall in love, Leonardo becomes distracted by her bracelet and then loses interest in her in favor of another painting he will do, *The Last Supper*. When Mona Lisa sees how distracted he becomes, she ceases to model for him and leaves him abruptly as she understands that he is more interested in his art, or rather the illusion that art provides, than in real people with real love. This is not dissimilar to Pierre Vidal's notions of art, beauty and invisibility in one of Verne's very last novels, *The Secret of Wilhelm Storitz* (*Le Secret de Wilhelm Storitz*, posthumously published in 1910).[20] At

---

18. This play will appear as *Mona Lisa* in a translation by Kieran O'Driscoll in the upcoming Palik Series volume *Worlds Known and Unknown*.

19. Pierre-André Touttain, editor, *Cahiers de l'Herne, Jules Verne* (Paris: Les Editions de l'Herne/Fayard, 1974), 23-56.

20. The 1910 publication of *The Secret of Wilhelm Storitz* was a text revised by Verne's son and literary executor, Michel Verne. In 1985, the original

the end of *Monna Lisa*, Leonardo declares that he prefers, as Verne biographer Herbert R. Lottman concludes, "the ideal image all poor poets carry in their heads" to the ups and downs of reality.[21] For Verne, the famous melancholic smile so familiar to the visitors of the Louvre, is a result of both scorn and pity for an artist who, according to Jean-Jules Verne, "placed his vision above earthly love."[22]

In this paradigm, la Guimard is doubly mature and strong as she both appreciates and is excited enough by David's art to champion him at the Rome Prize, but is also wise enough to know that true love should be honored. She understands that putting her own desires over a couple's happiness would in the end be a futile and empty pursuit. La Guimard is also more mature than Musset's portrayal of the famous ballet dancer La Camargo in one of his very first plays (written when he was nineteen years old but never produced during his lifetime), *Les Marrons au feu* (*Chestnuts in the Fire*), in which the beautiful dancer must choose between a handsome rogue whom she loves but who doesn't really care about her and an abbot who adores her but who is quite ugly.[23] Ultimately, she orchestrates a duel in which the rogue is killed by the abbot. While Musset's play in verse is replete with shipwrecks, costumes, violence and mistaken identity, Verne's *La Guimard*, in contrast, is a play in which wisdom triumphs over artistic narcissism and where the real beauty, as in *The Secret of Wilhelm Storitz*, is *within* rather than in appearance which is prone to illusion and disillusion.

In an article written by Gautier on Verne in the newspaper the *Moniteur Universel* in 1883, about Verne's imaginary voyages, Gautier urges his readers to forgo actually going to the theater after a disappointing season but rather to retreat to their armchairs instead where, if they could read a Verne novel, they would be able to travel endlessly in the comforts of their homes. "The show from their armchairs

---

manuscript from Jules Verne's own hand was published in France. Both of these versions have been translated, the Michel Verne text by I.O. Evans (Westport, CT: Associated Booksellers, 1963), and the Jules Verne text by Peter Schulman (Lincoln: University of Nebraska Press, 2011).

21. Lottman, *op. cit.*, 51.

22. Jean-Jules Verne, *Jules Verne* (Paris: Hachette, 1973), 47, 291-292, cited by Lottman, *op. cit.*, 52.

23. Alfred de Musset, *Les Marrons du feu*, in *Premières Poésies*, 1829-1835 (Paris: Charpentier, 1863), 23-67.

is the one best suited to such times," he declares, concluding his article with a ringing endorsement of Verne's amiable characters which, he says, should inspire one to go out and "spend a few hours with these fine companions in a desert of ice in a house of snow."[24] I would disagree with Gautier on one point, however: going to the theater is still a unique experience, and through the fine work of the Palik Series, my hope is that the plays in this collection not only find their way into readers' laps at home but that Verne's characters might finally get a chance to come alive and have their voices heard. Their home is on the stage for modern audiences to appreciate and enjoy.

– Peter Schulman
Norfolk, Virginia

---

[24]. Théophile Gautier, "Les Voyages imaginaires de M. Jules Verne," *Moniteur Universel*, 197 (July 16, 1866), reprinted in Touttain, *op. cit.*, 85.

An Excursion At Sea
A Light Comedy in One Act

CAST OF CHARACTERS

ANTOINE:	Captain of the *Passe-Partout*
CAPSTAN:	Boatswain of the *Passe-Partout*
LORD GRAY:	Owner of the *Saint-Dustan*
CORNBILL:	Lieutenant on the *Saint-Dustan*
LORD PAQUET:	Future son-in-law of Lord Gray
JACK:	Cook aboard the *Saint-Dustan*
GEORGES:	Cadet aboard the *Saint-Dunstan,* Anna's lover
LADY GRAY:	Lord Gray's wife
ANNA GRAY:	Lord Gray's daughter
LADY OSSULTON:	Lady Gray's cousin
FRENCH SAILORS	
ENGLISH SAILORS	

The action takes place on the bridge of the Saint-Dunstan, a leisure yacht belonging to Lord Gray

Le gabarier apprécia-t-il ces beautés naturelles? (Page 131.)

From *Mirifiques Aventures de Maître Antifer* (*Wonderful Adventures of Master Antifer*, 1894).

SCENE I.

LORD GRAY, CORNBILL.

LORD GRAY: Well, lieutenant!

CORNBILL: Getting back to what you just said, Milord. That cutter is a French smuggling vessel looking to drop off its merchandise on the Isle of Wight.

LORD GRAY: Are you quite sure about that, Cornbill?

CORNBILL: But can't you see that as long as the North East breeze was blowing, it had tacked so it could unload its bundles as soon as it could?

A cutter.

Carronade.

LORD GRAY: But how could it be that the presence of my yacht, the *Saint-Dunstan,* wasn't enough to make it run away?

CORNBILL: You see, Milord, with all due respect to Your Grace, he could see what he was running away from! The *Saint-Dunstan* is a cutter, just like the smuggler's vessel; it is the best rigged and scrubbed leisure boat in yacht society; in the most recent Plymouth races, it beat its fiercest competitor by a half-broadside; but it's not a war vessel after all!

LORD GRAY: Indeed it isn't! By King George, but if need be it would outwit any buccaneer along the coast! I'm not a sailor, but I have here eight lovely *carronade*[1] cannons that can speak loudly if the situation demanded it!

CORNBILL: I believe it, Milord; but I've already explained to you why the smuggler isn't concerned about any surprises coming his way from us! We are in no way at war with France, and this cutter, with its only slightly leaning masts that seem very French to me, would easily be able to pass through with its smuggled goods as long as it didn't accidentally make itself known to one of His British Majesty's cruisers.

LORD GRAY: He would have trouble doing that though. See, the wind has dropped, and when last seen, followed a calm spell with rough seas which can wear on a ship while preventing it from going any further than a buoy.

CORNBILL: This puts a damper on your excursion at sea, and I'm sure that Lady Gray, Anna Gray your charming daughter, Lady Ossulton, your respectable sister,

---

1. *Carronades* were little cannons that were initially melted down in the English town of Carron. They were powerful but had a short range.

« Qui sait ? » répondit Jean Taconnat. (Page 18.)

From *Clovis Dardentor* (1896).

	bitterly regret not being at your charming cottage in Plymouth!
LORD GRAY:	Misfortune and Fury! Mr. Cornbill, the wind was rather good this morning. There is no way we can keep it going.
CORNBILL:	See here, Milord, our spanker and fore-sail are turned-up on their brails! And at the slightest gust of wind, the jib, which his hanging like a torn rag, will warn us to stiffen our tacks![2]
LORD GRAY:	What should we do to pass the time? I would give a thousand guineas to find out! If melancholy strikes me, I beg you to throw me overboard, Mr. Cornbill.
CORNBILL:	Aye, aye, Milord.
LORD GRAY:	Mr. Jack! Mr. Jack! What on earth is Mr. Jack doing, is he without wind?

SCENE II.

LORD GRAY, CORNBILL, JACK.

JACK:	Milord.
LORD GRAY:	Well then, Master Jack, what about the provisions?

---

2. Verne uses 19th century technical nautical vocabulary here: "spanker" and "fore-sail" are translations for *brigantine* (the biggest sail from the front mast) and *misaine* (the big sail on the principal mast); "brail" is a translation of *cargues* which are the lighter ropes used to hoist the sails onto the foreyard in order to shield them from the wind; "jib" is a translation of *foc* (head sail) and "tacks" are translations of *amures* (tacks).

JACK: Alas! Milord, they are just about finished.

CORNBILL: As we are, are you aware of that, Master Jack?

LORD GRAY: Well, sir, what would we find here? A few scrawny chickens, a few very ordinary fish, a few pieces of rotten fruit! And for whom, for me, Lord Gray, member of Parliament, afflicted with two hundred thousand sterling in revenues! Ah! Mr. Cornbill, lieutenant on my yacht the *Saint-Dunstan!* I'm a very unhappy man!

JACK: I beg Your Grace's pardon, Milord, but that cutter could perhaps come to our rescue!

LORD GRAY: Master Jack, if that's the advice you're giving, you might as well go hang yourself.

JACK: Please excuse me, Milord! It's just that this vessel… is normally quite well stocked!

CORNBILL: Do you recognize it?

JACK: It's the *Passe-Partout*.[3] A French smuggling vessel, the very one with which Your Grace exchanged a bit of gunfire along the Plymouth coast.

LORD GRAY: What? That's the wretch who dared to land recently near my house in Plymouth?

JACK: The very one, Your Honor!

LORD GRAY: And who deprived your honor of an entire night's sleep.

---

3. Today, one cannot help but think of Verne's choice to name the smuggling vessel *Passe-Partout* in the context of the name of Phileas Fogg's manservant in *Around the World in Eighty Days*.

JACK: Yes! Your Grace!

CORNBILL: Master Jack is right, Milord!

LORD GRAY: Master Jack will light his ovens, and prepare the most splendid meal that has ever gone down a lord's trap, and from a cook's brain! He shouldn't worry about depleting his reserves! Before long we will enjoy fresh provisions! For which, Master Jack can look forward to not being hung today! Come on!

SCENE III.

LORD GRAY, CORNBILL.

CORNBILL: What are your intentions, Milord?

LORD GRAY: You were just saying that this French buccaneer would be rather embarrassed if a cruiser decided to arm its skiffs and directed them towards him.

CORNBILL: Without a doubt, Milord! This hopeless calm would prevent him from fleeing, and he would inevitably be captured!

LORD GRAY: But he would defend himself, I suppose, and it would at that point become a real attack!

CORNBILL: Quite the opposite, Milord, I assure you. These smugglers no longer have formidable arms at their disposal; flight is their greatest strategy for success, and the lightness and fineness of their ship are their greatest means for fleeing! Take a look at that cutter, look how open it is on the water, so tight and elevated up front, how its set of masts is both high and light at the same time, how the gigantic spank that stretches beyond its aft must make it race at fiery speeds! I'm sure it flies by at twelve knots with a good breeze behind it!

LORD GRAY: Well, sir, the *Saint-Dunstan* will give it a hard time!

From the novel *Les Enfants du capitaine Grant* (*The Children of Captain Grant*, 1868).

CORNBILL:	I agree with you, Milord, but this cutter is still a first-rate strider; it sacrificed everything for speed, and after all we don't see any brass cannons sticking their sharp heads through the scuttle-holes of his ship.
LORD GRAY:	Well then, Mr. Cornbill, come down with me for a minute and arm yourself to the teeth, and proceed to monitor that cutter's every movement!
CORNBILL:	Ahoy! Someone's here!

(*Georges arrives.*)

GEORGES:	Here I am, lieutenant!
CORNBILL:	Don't let that ship out of your sights, and put all our skiffs to sea.

SCENE IV.

GEORGES.

GEORGES:	(*By himself.*) What are their intentions? To unload their ladies perhaps! And me, who hasn't even dared speak to Miss Anna yet! She didn't recognize me in this disguise; it's true that I fled as soon as soon as I saw her coming, settling for looking at her in silence! And that old idiot that they intend for her, that Lord Packet! As a bold midshipman, I have to admit that I have so little courage! It's because I love her so much. Why does she have to belong to such a high family as Lord Gray's? Because she loves me! I think so!

The Verne maritime hero from *Le Chancellor* (*The Chancellor*, 1875).

SCENE V.

GEORGES, ANNA, LADY GRAY, LADY OSSULTON, LORD PACKET.

ANNA: Let's go! Come along, auntie! Come along mother!

LADY OSSULTON: Ah! We'll surely perish! The waves are waves are crashing all around us!

ANNA: But there is no wind at all.

LADY GRAY: Undoubtedly, cousin! And you are quite a fearful person for your age!

LADY OSSULTON: But at my age, we drown like any other person!

LORD PACKET: Undoubtedly! Undoubtedly! Oh! I'm so sick!

ANNA: What does this old lovebird think he looks like!

LORD PACKET: Miss Anna, my beautiful Miss Anna, Ah! I'm so sick!

LADY GRAY: Take some pastilles for your nausea!

LORD PACKET: I can't take anything! Oh! I'm so sick!

LORD OSSULTON: Alas! We're all going to perish! Aren't we sinking?

LADY GRAY: But cousin, but my future son-in-law, why don't you stop complaining and have a look at yourselves! Miss Ossulton is frightened to death seeing Lord Packet so ill, and Lord Packet is feeling even sicker seeing Miss Ossulton tremble!

Paganel parlait avec une animation superbe. (Page 45.)

From the novel *The Children of Captain Grant*.

ANNA: Why don't you just have a look around you! There is no danger to threaten you! Cousin, why don't you get on a more sailor-like footing, and you Lord Packet, get yourself a sailor's stomach as well! Look at me!

LADY OSSULTON: But are you aware, Miss Anna, that they say we run out of food!

LORD PACKET: Oh! Based on what I already consumed! I couldn't care less!

LADY OSSULTON: I think you are audaciously selfish, Milord!

LORD PACKET: Milady, I'm sea sick, and I beg you not to speak about anything else! What a great idea Lord Gray had to go out to sea in such weather!

LADY GRAY: What Lord Gray does is well done, Mr. Future Son-in-Law!

ANNA: Since I keep on repeating that we're in completely calm ….

LADY OSSULTON: Completely calm! Lost! Lost! We'll never see our dear homeland again: our supplies will completely run out! And we'll be reduced to eating each other! Where are my potatoes of yore and my steaks from yesteryear! Poor ladies, so weak and defenseless who are exposed to the voracity of our own sailors, our own parents, our own selves!

LADY GRAY: My dear cousin, you have such singular ideas at your age!

LORD PACKET: The fact is, Milady, that you will be eaten last; but it won't take me long to die, as my hearing is going, my stomach is going, everything's going! Ah! Ah! I'm really so sick!

Géricault's *The Raft of the Medusa*.

Verne's novel *The Chancellor* was also inspired by the painting of the *Medusa*.

LADY OSSULTON: We're right out of Gericault's *Raft of the Medusa!* And no ship anywhere on the horizon!

ANNA: On the contrary, auntie, take a look!

LADY OSSULTON: Take a look! Never! They're going to attack us and sink us, I'm sure! It's an enemy vessel! A Javanese pirogue! I can see some cannibals!

LORD PACKET: Milady, for God's sake, don't scream like that, you're making me twice as sick!

LADY OSSULTON: And you dear sir, do stop your shocking convulsions, it can be spread through the eyes!

LORD PACKET: Ah! I'm so sick!

LADY OSSULTON: Ah! We're all going to perish!

LADY GRAY: I can no longer take such a spectacle, fear and nausea will overtake me as well!

ANNA: Auntie, Milord! Be quiet for goodness' sake! Where is my father so he can reassure us all?

LADY OSSULTON: Your father! … That handsome sailor.

LADY GRAY: Milady, whatever Lord Gray does is well done.

ANNA: In that case, what happened to lieutenant Cornbill?

LADY OSSULTON: They abandoned us! The cowards!

LORD PACKET: Oh! Oh! I'm really so sick!

ANNA: (*Calling out to Georges.*) My friend, are we in any danger?

GEORGES: None at all, Miss Anna!

ANNA: (*To herself.*) That voice! It's him! Him!

LADY GRAY: Well, my daughter!

ANNA: Nothing…nothing…we have nothing to fear. (*To herself.*) As long as my father…

SCENE VI.

GEORGES, ANNA, LADY GRAY, LADY OSSULTON, LORD PACKET, LORD GRAY, CORNBILL, *sailors.*

(*Lord Gray and Cornbill come back up armed to the teeth!*)

LORD GRAY: Everybody on deck!

ANNA: What's going to happen?

GEORGES: (*To himself.*) She's recognized me.

LADY OSSULTON: Good God! We're sinking!

LORD PACKET: I'm feeling sicker and sicker.

LORD GRAY: See how our excursion can be prolonged indefinitely!…

LORD PACKET: Ouf!

LORD GRAY: And I'm on the verge of running out of supplies….

LADY OSSULTON: I won't be eaten, I won't be eaten!

LORD GRAY: Silence, my cousin…what was I saying, Cornbill?

Les passagers du *Chancellor*. (Page 4.)

From *The Chancellor*.

Juhel dirigea la lunette vers l'horizon. (Page 196.)

From *Wonderful Adventures of Master Antifer*.

CORNBILL:	And that we were about to run out of supplies…
LADY OSSULTON:	Ah! Lord!
ANNA:	Bravo, father!
LORD GRAY:	I'm quite pleased with this sentence, Cornbill. Do, let me have your attention for a minute, here by our port side ….
CORNBILL:	(*In a lower voice.*) Starboard!
LORD GRAY:	… Starboard, I mean, a ship, a brig…
CORNBILL:	A cutter ….
LORD GRAY:	… A cutter, I mean, that we know to be the *Passe-Partout*, a French smuggler ….
LADY OSSULTON:	Smuggler! The *Passe-Partout*! French! To me! Help! Take me to the bottom of the hold ….
LORD GRAY:	Cousin! Corbill, what do you think has gotten into my cousin all of a sudden?
CORNBILL:	I'm too much of your lieutenant to tell you that she's afraid, Milord.
LORD GRAY:	I feel exactly the same way! It's a shame that it's got to be my cousin, I would have attached her to a cannon! It adds a bit of a nautical quality to it.
CORNBILL:	I think the same way as Your Grace.
LORD GRAY:	Therefore, Mr. Cornbill and I, or rather, I and Mr. Cornbill, or even, I myself, we have decided that it would be appropriate to seize this schooner!

CORNBILL: Cutter!

LORD GRAY: Yes, cutter schooner! Schooner cutter, and to replace His Royal Majesty's cruisers for a bit.

ANNA: How my father…

LORD GRAY: It will look good in *The Times*.

LADY GRAY: What you do is well done, Milord.

LADY OSSULTON: What, you want to attack! But you'll be massacred, my cousin, and us along with you!

LORD GRAY: And where would the merit be if there were no dangers to confront, and what if these pirates don't fight until the death? Moreover, they have no weapons!

ANNA: But, my father, what have these poor folk done to you, for you to interfere with their business? They are the ones who are bringing you precious objects from France, and the majority of our jewels and lace have arrived through fraudulent means!

LORD GRAY: Because I say it, my girl, that these people have no weapons! The calm waters hold them captive.

LORD PACKET: What do you mean by calm, you call this calm?

LORD GRAY: Silence, aboard my ship!

ANNA: Why don't you leave these matters to our kingdom's police, it is not up to you, father, to make prisoners out of these people who have done you no harm, and who would willingly give you some food if you need some!

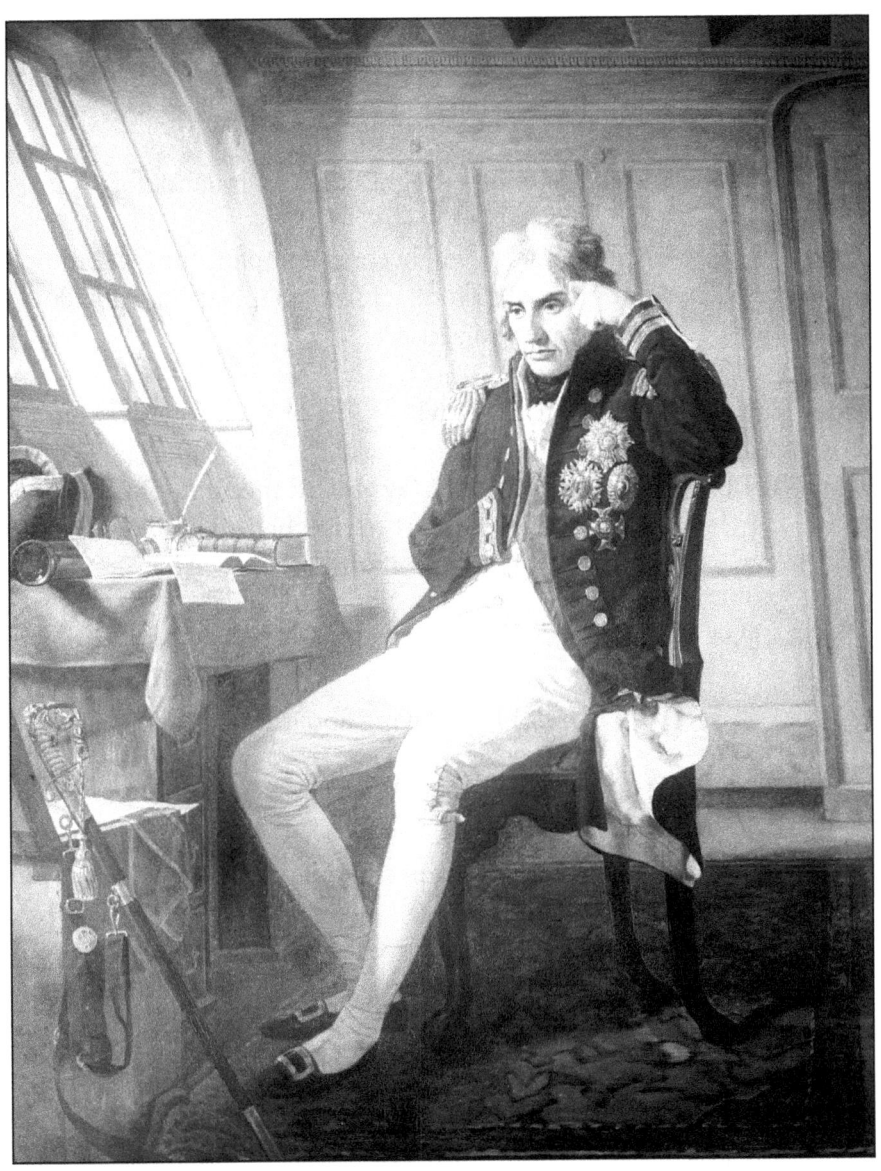

Admiral Nelson in his cabin aboard the *Victory*.

LORD GRAY: My girl, you are really your aunt's niece. Mr. Cornbill, are our skiffs fully armed?

CORNBILL: Yes, Milord.

LORD GRAY: Your best sailor will stay on board and the rest will accompany us. Lord Packet, you can chose to stay with these ladies or follow us!

LORD PACKET: I request to be brought back to dry land, forthwith.

LADY GRAY: Milord Packet will keep us company; go off, Milord, our glory calls you! ... remember Nelson, and allow me to give you a kiss.[4]

LORD GRAY: Very well, my lady!

CORNBILL: (*To Georges.*) You stay aboard the *Saint-Dunstan*, and if the winds start to rise, helped only by the foresail, you'll skim past the *Passe-Partout*.

GEORGES: Yes lieutenant!

ANNA: (*To herself.*) He's staying aboard!

LORD GRAY: Let's attack, lieutenant.

LADY OSSULTON: No, but we will sink while you are gone…

LORD PACKET: I positively demand to be let off on dry land, because I am too sick!

ANNA: Father, father! You're engaging in piracy now!

CORNBILL: The crew is waiting for you in the boats!

LORD GRAY: Let's go, Mr. Cornbill. Don't we need to line our boats with material so that we don't make any noise when we row, so that we can surprise this privateer?

---

4. Lord Horatio Nelson, Great Britain's most famous admiral who defeated the French navy at the battle of Trafalgar on October 21, 1805 and died during the battle. He famously said "England expects that every man will do his duty" before the battle and as he died, he asked his flag captain, Sir Thomas Hardy, to kiss him ("Kiss me, Hardy").

The *Victory* at sea.

The death of Nelson.

C'était un brick nommé *Macquarie*. (Page 435.)

From the novel *The Children of Captain Grant*.

CORNBILL: There's no need for that, Milord, this is the middle of the day!

LORD GRAY: I know but it would make it seem so nautical! Brave crew, cry out "long live the captain!"

THE SAILORS: Long live the Captain.

SCENE VII.

GEORGES, ANNA, LADY GRAY, LADY OSSULTON, LORD PACKET.

LADY OSSULTON: I can no longer bear witness to such a bloodbath!

LORD PACKET: As soon as there were fewer people on the boat, it's dancing even more and I'm going to have to give up the ghost!

LADY GRAY: Cousin, we would do well by praying for the success of our weapons!

ANNA: As long as my father doesn't repent for his impudent resolution!

GEORGES: (*To himself.*) Fear not, Miss Anna, for I am ready to give up my life for you!

LADY OSSULTON: All of you who surround me, do you know what awaits us? Apparently sinking isn't enough, nor dying of hunger or being devoured by Hottentots[5] or cannibalizing each other, now you have to lead us to slavery! But do you know what will become of us

---

5. The Hottentots were a name given to an African tribe known for their cannibalism in 18th and 19th century literature.

when we are given over to the brutality of a conquering crew? Oh! We haven't even reached the age of forty to get to this! I'm going back to my cabin, and I'm barricading myself in!

LADY GRAY: I'm following you, my sister, so that I can join my prayers to yours!

LORD PACKET: As for me, I'm going to put myself to bed! Make sure that a pail is brought to my cabin!

GEORGES: It will get there as soon as you do, Milord.

LORD PACKET: Oh! I'm so sick!

SCENE VIII.

GEORGES, ANNA.

ANNA: Here we are, by ourselves!

GEORGES: Miss Anna, I won't bother asking you if you recognized me. My love should excuse my conduct!

ANNA: You are completely forgiven, Georges.

GEORGES: That was the only way I could get near you. Even though I belong to a noble family, my modest ease forced me to stay away from you; I'm but a simple midshipman aboard the *Victory*, a ship in His Majesty's navy![6] And I can't compete with the high aristocracy that has graced your family's arm! Frankly, you must forgive the means with which my love has suggested I get closer to you, Miss Anna!

---
6. The *Victory* was part of Admiral Nelson's fleet during the battle of Trafalgar.

An Excursion At Sea

« Ne t'occupe pas tant de ta femme, Juhel. » (Page 411.)

From *Wonderful Adventures of Master Antifer*.

ANNA: I've already told you, Georges, my heart has no need to forgive you, as it loves you, but it isn't free to!

GEORGES: You gave it to someone else!

ANNA: No, but my father has!

GEORGES: In favor of Lord Packet!

ANNA: I don't see how you can call that a "favor"!

GEORGES: You mean you don't love him, Miss Anna?

ANNA: How could I?

GEORGES: Of course not! He's old, ridiculous, and ugly!

ANNA: No, Georges, you're the one I love, and any man with a heart in Lord Packet's shoes would have given up such outdated goals. I did everything to put a damper on his ambitions, but it's as though he were blind to it all, as though he understood nothing! I shudder to think about the outcome of all his efforts!

GEORGES: You see that we are in a miserable state, Miss Anna!

ANNA: I'm in a more pitiful state than you, Georges. I'm forced to exhibit borrowed joy and smiles on demand, as it is in not clashing with paternal designs that we can hope to win my father over! While you can sigh and cry all you like!

GEORGES: Miss Anna, is your mother just as unfavorable to us!

ANNA: My mother thinks that whatever my father does is just fine! When he so haughtily turned down your first request, Lady Gray applauded his decision;

when he officially introduced me to Lord Packet, my mother was delighted by his choice, and if Lord Gray ever went back to showing his best intentions toward you, my mother would be only to happy to have you as a son-in-law! Let's wait Georges!

GEORGES: Wait! But we'll run out of time. Without that, Miss Anna, with the hope of our love, I'll get there on high or I'll die getting there!

ANNA: Come now, Georges, some courage is needed now, and be careful not to clash with my father in respects to any of his decisions; I tremble at the thought that he might catch you hiding on board beneath these sailors clothes of yours! And how did you get here by the way?

GEORGES: I took advantage of a leave! Knowing that Lord Gray was thinking of going on an excursion at sea and that a few members of his crew missed the roll call, I offered to fill in for one of them, and I was accepted.

ANNA: But when he comes back…

GEORGES: When he comes back, he will be ready to go back to port, farewell then to all that happiness I was able to taste for a few days!

ANNA: Come on, Georges, tell me, my father is in no danger is he?

GEORGES: I don't know, Miss Anna, those smugglers who gamble with their lives defend themselves occasionally, and then…but the incident should be over by now. Indeed! There's a rowboat detaching itself from a side of the cutter!

ANNA: Oh! That was done without making a sound! Farewell, Georges, keep on looking at me, as I will only be able to look at you sometimes!

GEORGES: Your hand, Miss Anna!

ANNA: My God! Mother, Cousin, come quickly, we are triumphant! (*Yelling from a megaphone.*) Everyone on deck!

SCENE IX.

GEORGES, ANNA, LADY GRAY, LADY OSSULTON, LORD PACKET, JACK.

ANNA: Come let us join in Lord Gray's victory.

LADY OSSULTON: Finally! We won't die from starvation!

LADY GRAY: Can it be my noble husband who is coming towards us on the skiff?

ANNA: Undoubtedly Mother, don't you recognize his beautiful commander's uniform?

LORD PACKET: My goodness, I'm feeling a bit less sick!

LADY OSSULTON: Yes! That's him, accompanied by his lieutenant.

LORD PACKET: Pass me the spyglass, Miss Ossulton! Oh! Look how they're dancing! Here comes my nausea again.

LADY OSSULTON: Give me that spyglass, Milord! I can see some supply bundles that they are bringing us no doubt.

An Excursion At Sea   53

From *Seconde Patrie* (*Second Homeland,* 1900; Part 2: *The Castaways of the Flag* [Sampson Low edition, 1923].

« J'ai bien l'honneur de vous saluer, monsieur. » (Page 134.)

From *L'Agence Thompson and Co.* (*The Agency Thompson and Co.*, 1907).

From *Le Phare du bout du monde* (*The Lighthouse at the End of the World*, 1905 [Sampson Low edition, 1923])

GEORGES: (*To himself.*) That's strange, that's not at all lieutenant Cornbill's demeanor!

ANNA: (*To herself.*) It doesn't really look like my father!

LADY OSSULTON: I see some cuts of venison that appear to be a good omen!

LADY GRAY: Here they are!

JACK: That's good news, because I put the last of our steaks on the grill and we were about to be reduced to eating our shoelaces.

ALL: Here they are!

LADY OSSULTON: Three cheers for the victor!

GEORGES: Good God! What did I just see? A hatchet! Now it's my turn!

(*He jumps onto the parapet holding the hatchet.*)

SCENE X.

GEORGES, ANNA, LADY GRAY, LADY OSSULTON, LORD PACKET, JACK, ANTOINE, CAPSTAN, *sailors.*

GEORGES: Woe to the first one of you who…

ANTOINE: Be bold, boys!

(*Antoine, Capstan, the sailors rush towards Georges and disarm him.*)

LADY OSSULTON: Savages! Savages! I'm sure these people are naked!

CAPSTAN: Excuse me, My Lady, I has knickers!

LADY OSSULTON: Shocking! Shocking!

ANNA: And my father?

LORD PACKET: We're finished!

ANTOINE: Ladies and gentlemen, lend us your ears; we'll give them back to you in good shape! We are French and smugglers; we speak your language like your father and mother; there's a way for us to communicate then: the Milord commander of the *Saint-Dunstan* had the cheeky idea to capture the *Passe-Partout*; that was an act of piracy since he had neither a mission, nor letter of marque, moreover he was captured himself and is quite shamefaced.[7]

CAPSTAN: Like a porpoise who's broken his pipe!

ANTOINE: His lieutenant, his sailors and he himself are solidly docked at the bottom of our hold, and since Lord Gray wanted to take my ship, it's only normal that I take his!

GEORGES: This is infamy! Let go of me!

ANTOINE: Tie this gentleman up tightly! We'll settle up a little later!

ANNA: Milord smuggler.

ANTOINE: You are a sweet young lady, you that I would like to see decorating my cutter's bow, but silence in the ranks!

---

7. A letter of marque was a license allowing privateers to capture enemy vessels to be brought back to admiralty courts for condemnation and sale.

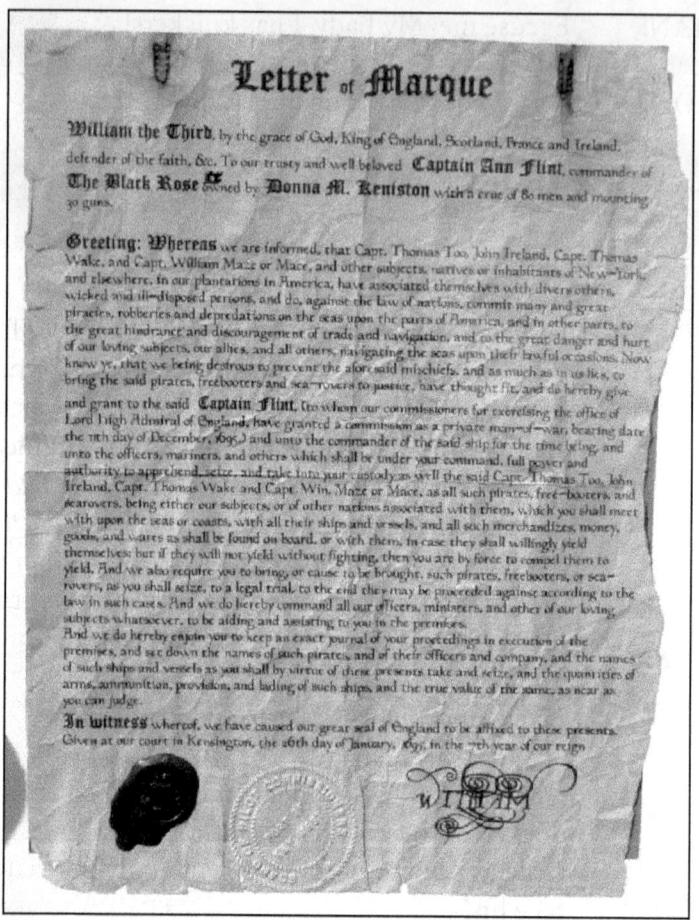

A letter of marque.

LORD PACKET: You can see in me a deeply ill man, sir!

ANTOINE: I am Milord Gray, and here is my lieutenant Cornbill; since we have his clothes! Be quiet!

CAPSTAN: Why don't we put him atop the mast as a lightning rod?

ANTOINE: Not yet, Capstan![8] But find a man of good will to exchange clothes with him! Hola! All you others,

---

8. Capstan's name (as his French one, Cabestan) refers to the vertical-axeled rotating device used on sailing ships used for winding rope or cable.

	bring down the bundles and put them in the mess hall!
LADY OSSULTON:	Mr…
ANTOINE:	Milord, for goodness' sakes. What do you want, old lady ….
LADY OSSULTON:	Old lady!
CAPSTAN:	She looks like an old razed pontoon that no longer has any curves!
LADY OSSULTON:	I am Lady Jane Gertrude Ossulton, young lady…
ANTOINE:	Be quiet or I'll send you to the kitchen to cook for us!
LADY OSSULTON:	Me, the kitchen…this is infamy, a horror! I'll complain! Get me the constable! The policemen!
CAPSTAN:	The old pontoon is lost at sea! This old lady has lost her bearings! Methinks we could open her pie hole wide with terror!
ANTOINE:	Silence, give us the mother or we'll strip you at the bottom of the hold!
LADY OSSULTON:	Ah! Good God! And I'm just a young lady, not even a woman yet!
ANTOINE:	Where is the ship's cook?
JACK:	I'm frightened to death.
CAPSTAN:	And for me a hawse-hole with tips made of old twine, with a marlinespike sauce, or I'll drink up your skull.[9]

---

9. Capstan's "recipe" is one made of nautical terms: "hawse-hole" (a small hole in

From the play *Les Enfants du capitaine Grant*
(*The Children of Captain Grant*, 1879).

JACK: Oh! Oh! Huh! I'm a dead man!

ANTOINE: Everyone line up, and I want you to recite all your physical and moral qualities, a thousand quakes of three hundred thousand tacks![10] Who are you, good lady?

LADY GRAY: Lord Gray's noble wife who breaths only for him ….

---

the hull of a ship to put a cable through); "gaskins" (small ropes); "marlinespike" (a tool to separate rope strands).

10. Colorful sailor cusswords similar to what Captain Haddock cries out in Hergé's *Tintin* when he is angry (see Philippe Valetoux's note in Verne's *Théâtre inédit*, *op.cit.*, 357).

ANTOINE:	That's for the best as it's my opinion he'll probably suffocate from all the coal down there in the hold; and this pretty girl?
ANNA:	Lord Gray's daughter, Sir, who considers you a coward for abusing your strength in relation to a few women!
ANTOINE:	Well said, she's got heart! A nice blade of girl! That's good. And this other one who is twisting and turning?
CAPSTAN:	Like a shark digesting a harpoon.
LORD PACKET:	I am a man who is very ill, Lord Packet, Miss Anna Gray's intended!
ANTOINE:	Ah! This old jokester! A future husband!
CAPSTAN:	This old man doesn't have many years left in him![11]
ANTOINE:	This pretentious fool! A few strikes from an ox's nerve between the shoulders will make him swallow his illness.[12] And this one here?
LADY OSSULTON:	A respectable lady.
ANTOINE:	Known! So how goes it? Very well! We don't hold any maidens of that age and, with the exception of the beautiful Miss, no maidens are allowed on board!
LADY OSSULTON:	Please respect what is most dear to me!

---

11. Verne uses an archaic sailor's phrase here *"une sorte de cachalot qui n'a pas de vergue de rechange!"* (a toothed-whale that doesn't have much yard to spare!)

12. Verne is referring to a type of hard stick made from the cervical ligaments of an ox's or horse's rear. It was dried and prepared to be used as a riding crop (Valetoux in Verne, *Théâtre inédit, op.cit.,* 357).

CAPSTAN: Do you see that old rusty blunderbuss over there that shoots off before we pull the trigger!

ANTOINE: Enough chatter! Everyone swallow their tongues! Everyone in the wardroom! As for this lad who almost hacked us to death, let's tie him up in the bows! Come on, everyone under the bridge, and prepare to obey the orders of Commander Lord Gray.

GEORGES: (*To himself.*) My God! Save her!

ANNA: (*To herself.*) We'll see! We'll see!

CAPSTAN: Everyone all at once: Long live the skipper!

ALL: Long live the skipper!

SCENE XI.

ANTOINE, CAPSTAN.

ANTOINE: Well my dear old Capstan, could anything more felicitous happen to us?

CAPSTAN: The fact is that we were there, going no faster than a buoy, and all our contraband lace, and our old cognac risked not getting to land anytime soon.

ANTOINE: And thanks to the imprudent boastfulness of that whippersnapper of a Lord, here we are out of a jam.

CAPSTAN: How then? Let the devil hang me if I understand you!

ANTOINE:	Didn't you see that the current was driving the cutter towards the island?[13]
CAPSTAN:	And even more, we are hardly a mile out, captain.
ANTOINE:	Well then old bean, we're going to be wildly content; we'll mystify Lord Gray, we'll scare the living daylights out of his illustrious family who take us for cannibals, and we'll cheat customs! That's all we'll do!
CAPSTAN:	I understands the beginning, that's already done, but not the end!
ANTOINE:	Listen to me; we've moved merchandise aboard the *Saint-Dunstan*. The cutter's skiffs are neither compromising nor suspicious. Yet, you're going back on land accompanied by the mother, the cousin, and the intended.
CAPSTAN:	A funny kind of good for nothin'; haven't seen anyone like him before! Wanting to live with such a beautiful lass like Miss Anna![14]
ANTOINE:	Pretty blade of girl! What a coronation!
CAPSTAN:	What a figure-head! What hawse-holes![15] Am I wrong?
ANTOINE:	Don't talk to me about that, Capstan! What a pretty carcass, all doweled and lined in brass!

---

13. Verne uses the word *drosser* which is used when a boat drifts irreparably towards land no matter its speed.

14. Once again Capstan speaks in pure nautical terminology: *Vouloir aborder par le travers une jolie goélette comme la Miss Anna* literally means "wanting to board a pretty schooner like Miss Anna abeam …."

15. Capstan uses nautical imagery in a sexual manner here.

From the play *The Children of Captain Grant*.

CAPSTAN: And what a lazaretto of a heart, where I bet one could find some nice appetizing things; I would love to tack about with her![16]

ANTOINE: Shush! Old man, we're buccaneers, but men of honor, and French! A thousand weathervanes, I'm telling the truth, am I not! Ah! Here we are: you come down with these three individuals, and a few of our sailors who are already informed about the matter and who are in the middle of carrying out a load.

CAPSTAN: Which one again?

---

16. *"je courrais bien des bordées de conserve avec elle!"* Capstan is referring to the way boats can run parallel to each other during manoeuvers or follow the same navigation route.

ANTOINE:	Can't you see that they are stuffed with lace underneath their garments and loaded with bottles! Let people think that they're actually the Lord's family so that they can pass by without receiving some nice gunshots as we would get and that they have everything at the correspondent's and bring them aboard!
CAPSTAN:	And what if they scream bloody murder once on land and that they tell everybody about our little show!
ANTOINE:	You joker! I'm holding hostages! The Lord and the lieutenant, right here aboard my ship! And here the young Missy!
CAPSTAN:	Ah, the famous captain! I understands you!
ANTOINE:	Yes, I'll speak a tad with her; she'll hide all sorts of nonsense, but that's all beneath me.
CAPSTAN:	And the individual who is getting corrected over there?
ANTOINE:	Oh! He's got plenty of heart for an Englishman; we'll let go of all of that once our little farce has played itself out! Ah that, they're already washed up! They put up some resistance, but our mates are talented chambermaids; and they wouldn't utter a word about it.
CAPSTAN:	I hear some balking going on over there!
ANTOINE:	Let the carnival commence!

SCENE XII.

ANTOINE, CAPSTAN, LADY OSSULTON, ANNA, LORD PACKET, JACK, *sailors*.

LADY GRAY: Oh! Lord! Me, the noble wife of Lord Gray.

LADY OSSULTON: Me, who is allied with the reigning race by men!

LORD PACKET: Me, me, one of the most influential members of the High Chamber of the English Parliament!

LADY GRAY: And to think, you loaded us up with contraband!

LORD PACKET: And decked me out with bottles of brandy!

LADY OSSULTON: And saw myself undressed by male and villainous hands! I'll die from it!

ALL: It's an indignity! A horror! Shocking!

JACK: Who can tell me what breaded poultry breasts with asparagus tips are?

LADY GRAY: I hope, Mr. …

ANTOINE: I am Milord Gray; please call me your dear husband.

LADY GRAY: I hope, my dear husband that you will go no further with this irreverent joke!

LADY OSSULTON: And you will punish the rebels that laid an insolent hand upon my charms.

ANTOINE: Silence among the ranks or I'll block off the cannon of whomever doesn't swallow their bluff.

ANNA:	You are a coward, sir!
GEORGES:	(*In the background.*) You are a coward!
JACK:	(*To Packet.*) What's this hawse-hole with tips made of old twine, with a marlinespike sauce?
ANTOINE:	Alright, go knock the block and tackle from the yard-arm of the top-sails, and send me a girtline. That man will be hanged within the hour!
ANNA:	My God! I'm dying!
ANTOINE:	Take the young lady towards the back; but it's highly unusual. Is everything already prepared in the row-boat?
CAPSTAN:	Yes, Captain!
ANTOINE:	(*To Capstan.*) Lieutenant Cornbill, you and three sailors will accompany the three passengers; you'll make sure that they don't say a word; at the slightest gesture, stab them; you'll go to my correspondent; and these gentlemen and ladies will be so good as to give him all the lace that they are lined with, and then they'll come back aboard.
LADY GRAY:	Never! Contraband!
LADY OSSULTON:	Us! Buccaneers!
LORD PACKET:	If I weren't so sick, I would box with you!
ANTOINE:	Thank you, I sell applications of English lace, but I don't receive them! Onwards! And don't forget that at the slightest sign of treason, I have Miss Anna, her father, etc. as hostages; that I'll blow everything up as soon as I get back to my own ship!

LADY OSSULTON: This is the end of the world!

CAPSTAN: Grab your child, mother.

(*He hands her a baby doll made up of different herbs.*)

LADY OSSULTON: A child! My own!

CAPSTAN: Indeed! One who won't cry on the way, given that he is made of pine wood, and that he has brandy in his veins!

LADY OSSULTON: Never! Me, a child? A maiden!

ANTOINE: There are no maidens on my ship.

CAPSTAN: Come now, mother, take that onto your bosom if you can so that you can at least have a taste of the sweetness of maternity once in your life. Everybody else, forward.

(*The sailors go down into the skiff.*)

LADY OSSULTON: I will never climb down from the deck. A stairway! I want a stairway!

ANTOINE: Let's have some respect for the gender! Clear off this chair, the rest of you.

(*The sailors attach a chair to a sprig of girtline, Lady Gray sits down on it and groans. They haul her over and drop her down into the row boat.*)

LORD PACKET: I'm next since I'm ill.

CAPSTAN: Come now! A sailor like you!

(*He takes him by the shoulders, and slumps him in half into the rowboat.*)

LADY OSSULTON: God! This will be the death of me, Lord!

CAPSTAN: Your turn, mother, take care of your child.

(*The sailors have fun hoisting Lady Ossulton who screams in terror, before they lower her into the boat.*)

ANTOINE: Bon voyage, Capstan, and look after the grain!

CAPSTAN: We'll be back in fifteen minutes, captain.

JACK: Great God, who can tell me what breaded poultry breasts with asparagus tips are?

SCENE XIII.

ANTOINE, ANNA.

ANTOINE: (*Alone.*) The lovely Miss! Does she have feelings for the lad that she fainted when we spoke of the noose?

ANNA: (*Going towards him.*) Sir, you wouldn't really put him to death would you?

ANTOINE: And what business is it of yours, Miss Anna?

ANNA: Sir, you wouldn't want the blood of an innocent man to tarnish the bridge of your ship would you?

ANTOINE: But you sure thought you saw the color of mine!

ANNA: But you were guilty!

ANTOINE: Really, Miss Anna! You need our business which is so squeaky honest I don't have to spell it out for you.

You are wearing lace and trinkets for which we risk our freedom every day; your illustrious gentlemen get drunk on wine and brandy that we pass on to them at great risk and peril to ourselves; and as if it weren't enough that we have English coast-guard vessels and cruisers on our backs, a Lord, a member of Parliament, just as a true police officer, to have fun rather than to enforce the law, comes without any orders to do so, without any letter of marque, without any destination, declare himself master of my ship, and when I defend myself, when I want to retaliate, I'm the guilty one!

ANNA: My father was wrong, sir, and I did everything I could to dissuade him from his project; but he didn't listen to me at all, and it's too late for remorse.

ANTOINE: And so what are you asking of me then, Miss Anna?

ANNA: To show mercy on this man; all he did was his duty by defending us.

ANTOINE: That's impossible.

ANNA: Nonetheless, I saw a good and humane person in you, Sir, and I wasn't wrong was I?

ANTOINE: So why do you take such an interest in this sailor?

ANNA: He is a man, sir.

ANTOINE: Ta ta ta ta!
(*To himself.*)
The pretty girl will not admit to what I saw. Let's see what happens.
(*Loudly.*)
It's a lad with a lot of courage in fact, and my anger does not make me unjust.

ANNA:	Oh indeed, sir!
ANTOINE:	His manners show that he is from a class that is superior to that of a simple sailor.
ANNA:	That is not the case, sir, he is a young man who is a member of the crew.
ANTOINE:	No doubt, and that is why I must act with severity or my men won't obey me any longer! Besides which, I have no choice.
ANNA:	Sir, please have mercy, I beg of you!
ANTOINE:	Do you love him?
ANNA:	No, sir, but I suffer. Yes, mercy!
ANTOINE:	There are no other men here besides Mr. Ossulton and him: you choose!
ANNA:	Mr. Ossulton?
ANTOINE:	Yes, I see, it's your intended!
ANNA:	Oh! That means nothing to me.
ANTOINE:	Huh?
ANNA:	I don't know what I'm saying, sir. Mercy, I beg of you, mercy!
GEORGES:	Pick yourself up, Miss Ann, don't lower yourself before this man!
ANNA:	Oh! Georges!

ANTOINE: (*To himself.*) She's such a stubborn little one, we'll see in a bit.

ANNA: Sir, what will you do with us after your expedition?

ANTOINE: We'll make contraband.

ANNA: Sir!

ANTOINE: Aren't you making some already, a bit of love contraband perhaps?

ANNA: Me! Mercy! Mercy!

ANTOINE: It is my honor to greet you, Miss Anna.

SCENE XIV.

ANNA, *alone.*

ANNA: Oh! My God! What shall I do? Poor Georges! Where did his love for me lead him! There he is, in chains! And soon…I'm losing my head, and yet this French pirate doesn't seem cruel! And yet… but Georges can't die! It's impossible! Young, brave, generous, it's for wanting to defend us that he risked his life, and now, he is about to lose it! But I'm going mad! My father! Where is my father? Prisoner! I'm surrounded by enemies! Oh! My Georges! Forgive me! Since I'm the one who is responsible for your death. Oh! I'll save him! I'll save him!

From *Wonderful Adventures of Master Antifer.*

SCENE XV.

ANNA, JACK.

JACK: Alas! Alas! Who can tell me ....

ANNA: Jack! What's on your mind!

JACK: Breaded poultry breasts with asparagus tips.

ANNA: Do you have a heart?

JACK: Not for two pence!

ANNA: Oh! My God, alone, alone! You wouldn't have the courage to cut Georges free would you?

JACK: What's this Georges?

ANNA: That young sailor who's chained to the ship's bow.

JACK: Faith in Jack, that's an idea that would never come to me! For example!

ANNA: You're a coward.

JACK: No, Milady, I'm a mess-hall cook.

ANNA: Give me that knife!

JACK: Never! I need it! Do you want to have my throat slit!

ANNA: Give it over!

JACK: I'm going to dive head first into my boiler!

SCENE XVI.

ANNA, JACK, ANTOINE.

ANTOINE: How's it going? Going well! So, Master Jack, now's the time to serve it while it's hot!

JACK: I'll serve myself!

ANTOINE:	Here's the rowboat coming back. Everything went as planned, all that's left to do is celebrate, with such a splendid meal, the outcome of such a grave affair!
JACK:	Yes, Milord.
ANTOINE:	We shall set the table on the bridge, if the weather is nice, and by the way, I'm not angry for having an eye on everything! I welcome you, Miss Anna; how is your appetite?
ANNA:	Oh, I feel myself trembling.
ANTOINE:	I wager that this rascal Jack will be surpassed.
JACK:	Surpassed? Milord!...
ANTOINE:	Be especially careful with what I ordered from you, eh! That smelt mayonnaise with the oyster sauce!
JACK:	Excuse me, Milord! They were breaded!
ANTOINE:	I think this jokester is answering me.
JACK:	Approximated eel excess with a hindoustani sauce.
ANTOINE:	Ah! Here they come! Miss Ossulton is all red, and Lord Packet is all white. Ahoy, from the rowboat!
VOICES:	Ahoy! The rowboat from the *Saint-Dustan,* lieutenant Cornbill!
ANTOINE:	That prankster Capstan! How well he plays his role! Draw the children alongside and show respect towards the ladies!

SCENE XVII.

ANNA, JACK, ANTOINE, CAPSTAN, LADY GRAY, LADY OSSULTON, LORD PACKET, *sailors*.

CAPSTAN: Pass the nutmeg, captain: the trick has been played.

ANTOINE: Thank you buccaneers and lady smugglers, you have earned all my thanks!

LADY GRAY: Shame, horror, infamy, atrocity!

LADY OSSULTON: They took me for a mother! And they complimented me on my newborn!

CAPSTAN: The fact is that you could very well change figureheads, but not you' respect

LORD PACKET: This nausea that had left me on land has suddenly come back with a vengeance!

ANTOINE: Did everything go well?

CAPSTAN: Without a hitch! We threw all the sails out, the comrade was, as one might say, the topsail and Madame, the foremast! We could have landed on some custom agents! But more often! They greeted Mrs. Lord Gray until their backbones broke and they complimented the little lady on her contraband mustard.

LADY OSSULTON: Contraband, no doubt.

CAPSTAN: I thinks it! You didn't get it through a legitimate marriage did you? For when we went to the correspondent, the ladies wore their underwear very low!

LADY OSSULTON: Oh, oh, yuk!

CAPSTAN:	And there, we allowed ourselves to spool them properly, no more no less than a cotton bobbin, seen as it was turning like a capstan which is my *nom de guerre*; as the company knows that I calls myself François Bidet, known as the artichoke gone to seed like that little mother over there by my sides!
ANTOINE:	And nothing happened outside of our little show?
CAPSTAN:	Nothing captain; that wise-guy who's twisting his stomach like a toothed whale that ate its bluff pretended to stay ashore, when I punched him at the bottom of his inexpressible, as we say, and I slipped his cable throwing him onto the rowboat, he might have gotten the lights punched out of him, he still thought he was the bees-knees.
ANTOINE:	Let's toast to the success of our enterprise and I invite this honorable company t'share our modest meal!
CAPSTAN:	(*To Jack.*) Well then, Master Jack, have you thought about my marinade of hallucination grist?
ANTOINE:	How come the table's not set?
CAPSTAN:	To the stoves, Jack the Fool, or I'll haul you down to the bottom of the hold with a slap.
LORD PACKET:	Captain, I ask your permission to retire to my cabin.
ANTOINE:	More often!
LORD PACKET:	Taking care of my health demands it!
ANTOINE:	Aha, do you realize you have one hell of a mug for a lover?

LORD PACKET: Yes, Milord, I have one hell of a mug, as you put it so elegantly, and that is why…

ANTOINE: Come on now! You'll eat on the go, it'll get you back on your feet.

LORD PACKET: It is physically impossible for me to eat anything on the go or otherwise!

CAPSTAN: And you'll take it on the nose, which will make you give you a funny look like a caiman with glasses.[17]

LORD PACKET: No doubt; I think, esteemed lieutenant, that if a caiman were to wear glasses…

ANTOINE: Come on! Enough of this chatter! Miss Anna, you know that if you prefer to watch Lord Packet hang, all you have to do is say so. You're not answering? A person who answers nothing gives his tacit approval!

LORD PACKET: For example! Help! Ah, I feel so sick! Miss Ossulton!

LADY OSSULTON: Have you quite finished tugging at my skirts. You are all too happy to die. If I had a knife, why I'd imitate Lucrece!

CAPSTAN: At y'r service, old lady.

ANTOINE: Capstan, advance on my order.

(*They chat.*)

ANNA: Mother! This is horrible!

LADY GRAY: What do you want my girl! If there were a need to save this young man!

---

17. "Caiman" can literally mean *caiman* or in sixteenth-century slang, a highwayman.

ANNA: Oh! I would die!

LADY OSSULTON: If I don't die of shame, I'll die of hunger!

LORD PACKET: And me for having eaten! Oh! Oh!

ANTOINE: And so the north west breeze is beginning to lift and it won't be long before we scram.

CAPSTAN: Yes, captain, especially since the position of our cutter is already suspicious! But you've agreed on a signal so that Milord can come back on board.

ANTOINE: Yes. We'll half-mast the flag! And he'll come with his lieutenant. Then we'll say hello to the company, and once aboard, we'll get rid of the English sailors!

CAPSTAN: Such a nice load, eh!

ANTOINE: I'll wager that everybody won't be unhappy on board; dinner!

JACK: I'm a dead man.

LADY GRAY: Horror! Infamy! Shame!

LADY OSSULTON: Having been a maiden up until this age in order to…

LORD PACKET: My last hour has arrived!

ANTOINE: Dinner! A thousand quakes, and woe to the laggards. I'm not inviting you so that you can have fun, by thunder, but to see your funny faces that you'll put on while you eat at my table! Not bad, Milord, not bad.

CAPSTAN: Long live joy and trifles; death to the Brits[18] and onward with mother lummox[19]! I'm happier than a puppy! Well then, you old man over there who seems to be sucking on razor blade, do we have to stuff food down your throat?

LORD PACKET: Spare me, esteemed lieutenant, as I am to be greatly pitied.

ANTOINE: By thunder and Elmo's fire, you can eat to your heart's content and you're still yapping; here's yar table up to your eyeballs in front of a partridge *salmis*[20] and a crayfish bisque, and you're complaining! A little later, you'll be eating an approximated eel excess with a hindoustani sauce, and you're still not happy! What would you have said then if I had marched you up to the top of the mainmast with two cannon balls on each foot, and a big mast through your head?

LORD PACKET: I wouldn't have said a thing, Milord…

ANTOINE: Enough, and let's drink! Well then, charming Miss, you're not unclenching your teeth! As you please! But let's drink!

LADY OSSULTON: The wretches are getting drunk! What will become of us? Me, me, the maiden!

CAPSTAN: I would bet that my neighbor feels like a kiss from her neighbor!

---

18. Verne uses a term that dates back to the hundred year war, the *godons*, a derivative of the "goddams."
19. *Godichon* would be a derivative of *godiche* which means "stupid woman" in French slang, but it is also a play on words with *godon* the euphemism for the British.
20. Ragout or casserole.

LADY OSSULTON: Bite your tongue!

CAPSTAN: Allow me to push my cheek to the left, and if you'd like, I're be be the father of your child.

LADY OSSULTON: Stop! Horror!

ANTOINE: Dinner! And let's drink some good and old wine! Ah, ah! The *Saint-Dunstan's* lazaretto seems quite docked to me.

CAPSTAN: It's as though we were swallowing paradise and the angels with it, and that the seraphs are tickling your throat while they're at it!

ANTOINE: To be served hot, Master Jack! Well then, Lord Packet, you're not eating?

LORD PACKET: I cannot!

ANTOINE: Why don't you eat something!

LORD PACKET: Impossible.

ANTOINE: You will eat, do you understand me? By a thousand portholes, you'll eat or you'll be hanged.[21] You'll die ….

LORD PACKET: Esteemed captain, I would prefer to eat, but it will boil down to the same thing.

CAPSTAN: Come now, a bit of enthusiasm please! If there weren't ladies present, I would belt out the song about Mother Canu, who became a widow on the eve of her nuptials.

ANTOINE: In that case, I'm gonna treat ya to some couplets from the handsome sailor!

---

21. *Mille sabords* literally means "a thousand portholes" but it's an old sailor's cuss.

CAPSTAN: Only if you applaud the commander.

ANTOINE: And that you cry out "Long Live France!"

                "Merry sailors,
                Jump onto the top mast
                To look for the dune
                Amidst the seas,
                Alert, kiddies, alert!
                The sky is blue, the sea is green.

                By leaving the shipboard
                You will hardly see
                Crying in the port
                Your old mother.
                During her sad adieu
                To the Saintly Virgin
                he made a vow
                To light a candle
                If her young son
                Saved from the storm
                Would come back home
                Come back to shore.
                For more than one lover
                Sobbing for his promised one
                Will swear his oath
                To the crazy breeze
                And curse fate
                And its casting off.
                And through the porthole
                That flees the shore,
                From loving her so much
                He swore his oath.
                The ship ships.

                Since everything is ready
                We dash off at thirteen,
                The master swore

An Excursion At Sea

From *Seconde Patrie*, 1900 (*Second Homeland*, 1905; Part 1: *Their Island Home* [Sampson Low edition, 1923].

Sailors singing below decks.

> That he could swim with ease
> And of his four fingers,
> Increased by his thumb,
> He slapped the sailor boy in the head
> Thirteen times.
> Our [code of honor]
> Prevents us from folding our sails
> Nor our jib or top sail,
> We are the swimming cast-offs.
>
> Merry sailors,
> Jump onto the top mast
> To look for the dune
> Amidst the seas,
> Alert, kiddies, alert!
> The sky is blue, the sea is green."[22]

---

22. This is a modified version of Verne's "Chanson des Gabiers" ("Song of the Topmen") found in an edition of Verne's unpublished poems (*Poésies inédites*. Paris: le Cherche Midi, 1989, pp. 55-57) written in December, 1847. A topman was a sailor in charge of all the sails.

ALL:	Long live the commander, long live France!
ANTOINE:	Come now, let's have some joy! I sing and nobody laughs, I swear and nobody laughs, I laugh and nobody laughs. For example! Ah I see you are not prone to jokes. Well then, enough chatter, enough laughter; let's think about our affairs. For desert, I will treat you to a dish that I thought up all by myself.
JACK:	Ouf!
ANTOINE:	Is the rope ready?
CAPSTAN:	Yes, captain.
JACK:	I'm a dead man!
ANTOINE:	Bring the convict forward.

SCENE XVIII.

ANNA, GRAY, ANTOINE, CAPSTAN, LADY GRAY, LADY OSSULTON, LORD PACKET, GEORGES, *sailors*.

GEORGES:	Above all, sir, I have one favor to ask of you.
ANTOINE:	What is it?
GEORGES:	The favor of not insulting me and letting me die without delay.
ANTOINE:	Your wish is my command!
ANNA:	Mercy! Mercy, sir!

LADY GRAY: My daughter! My daughter!

ANTOINE: Enough chatter! Since you can't take a joke, leave me alone.

ANNA: I beg you, sir, mercy or I'll die at your feet!

ANTOINE: The rules of the navy dictate that, during each execution, we lower the flat at half-mast! Proceed, lieutenant.

"I am getting sicker and sicker!," from the novel *The Children of Captain Grant*.

GEORGES:	Farewell, Miss Anna. Thank you for your prayers; but humiliate yourself no further as death will be very sweet for me.
ANNA:	My God!
CAPSTAN:	Everything's ready, captain!
ANTOINE:	As a favor to the young mother, I'm resurrecting that law that says that any woman who wishes to marry a man condemned to death will save the life of that man!
ANNA:	Oh! Thank you! Thank you!
LADY GRAY:	My daughter!
ANTOINE:	Well!
LADY OSSULTON:	Why this young man's not so bad, he seems noble and distinguished.
ANTOINE:	Well then! Carry out my orders, lieutenant!
ANNA:	Mother! Georges!
LADY OSSULTON:	And I'm so compromised! I'll marry him, sir!
ANNA:	Oh!
ANTOINE:	You!
CAPSTAN:	Her!
ANTOINE:	But you're already married!
LADY OSSULTON:	Me?

From *The Agency Thompson and Co.*

CAPSTAN: And this kid?

LADY OSSULTON: Infamy!

ANTOINE: You're married!

LADY OSSULTON: Never, I tell you!

ANTOINE: What thunder! They prattle when I speak! They reason when I say something! You're married, again.

LADY OSSULTON: Great God, with whom? So I'm married without ever noticing it.

ANTOINE:	Married to that contorting individual.
LORD PACKET:	Oh! I am getting sicker and sicker!
LADY OSSULTON:	But…
ANTOINE:	You're married, by a thousand thunders, and kiss your husband or I'll hang the both of you!
CAPSTAN:	What a beautiful couple! Two old carcasses.
ANTOINE:	No one is claiming the prisoner?
ANNA:	Yes, sir, I will marry him! I'll marry him not to save his life but because I love him and he loves me!
LADY GRAY:	My daughter!
ANNA:	Mother, this is Georges River, an officer of His Royal Majesty.
LADY GRAY:	Him!
ANTOINE:	Miss Anna, you cannot consent to this marriage by yourself; does Lady Gray give her word that it shall take place?
LADY GRAY:	Yes, sir!
ANNA:	Milord Gray, Madame!
ANTOINE:	Release the prisoner!
GEORGES:	Oh! Miss Anna!
ANNA:	My Georges!

ANTOINE: Let's pretend that we had always acted in good faith, my children…

ANNA *and* GEORGES: So it was ….

ANTOINE: Shush!

CAPSTAN: Lord Gray, lieutenant Cornbill!

SCENE XIX.

ANNA, JACK, ANTOINE, CAPSTAN, LADY GRAY, LADY OSSULTON, LORD PACKET, GEORGES, LORD GRAY, CORN-BILL.

LORD GRAY: I'm home, at last!

ANTOINE: Yes Milord! And your few moments in captivity will teach you to meddle in what concerns you. Let me introduce you to Lady Gray, Lord Packet, and his wife Miss Ossulton – all in fine shape.

CAPSTAN: And their child.

LORD GRAY: For example!

ANTOINE: And midshipman Georges River.

LORD GRAY: You? Here?

ANTOINE: And his wife, Miss Anna Gray!

LORD GRAY: Never!

From *The Agency Thompson and Co.*

ANTOINE: The wind is lifting, Milord; why don't you come to France? Your daughter, by marrying Georges, has saved him from the jaws of death!

LORD GRAY: From death!

ANTOINE: Yes, because he defended your daughter, your ship and he almost killed me.

LORD GRAY: So he really is my son-in-law!

ANTOINE: That's what I said! Good bye, let's set sail, my day was well spent!

GEORGES: Milord!

ANNA: My father!

LORD PACKET: Now I'm really going to be sick!

LADY OSSULTON: He's so ugly!

CAPSTAN: You're marrying a real porpoise here.

ANTOINE: When I said that there were no ladies on my ship!

THE END

The Thousand and Second Night

CAST OF CHARACTERS:

THE SULTAN OF PERSIA
SCHEHERAZADE, THE SULTANA
DINARZADE: Her sister.
HASSAN: A young Kalendar prince and favorite of the Sultan.

Music by Aristide Hignard.

The theater represents the interior of a harem in the Sultan's palace in Isphahan in Persia.

In the back, there is a platform with the Sultan's bed on it. Oriental luxury. A dimly lit night light. Scents are burning from the incense-burners. Carpets, drapes, etc.

SCENE I.

THE SULTAN, THE SULTANA.

(*The sultan is lying down and sleeping, the sultana is also sleeping, stretched at his feet on a lower platform. A soft music plays as they sleep.*)

SCENE II.

THE SULTAN, THE SULTANA, DINARZADE

DINARZADE: The sultan sleeps and the sultana
Shielded from profane glances
Seems to continue to pursue a dream of love!
Let's wake them up before daybreak.
(*Leaning towards the sultana.*)

My sister the hours are quick
To flee your meeting.
Tell us one of those tales
You tell so well.

THE SULTAN: (*Wakes up and sees the sultana.*)
Sheherazade! Ah! How beautiful she is!
The night
Takes flight
A new dawn is here!

This night
Is the thousand and first
Ever since love led
The one I love close to my heart.
To delay the day

>   Its next return
>   Am I not like Allah himself!
>
>   Ever since love led
>   The one I love close to my heart
>   This night
>   Is the thousand and first.

DINARZADE: A soft light has already descended from the heavens!
The day will soon be born.

THE SULTAN: Well, join your voice to your masters'!
That my dear sultana may finally open her beautiful eyes.

TOGETHER:

THE SULTAN	DINARZADE
My child, the hours are quick	My sister, the hours are quick
To flee your meeting	To flee your meeting
Tell us one of those tales	Tell us one of those tales
You tell so well!	You tell so well!

THE SULTANA: What! I was still sleeping and, I'm sure
Your Highness was waiting for me to wake up.

THE SULTAN: I was admiring your sweet sleep!

THE SULTANA: An especially sweet sleep this night, I swear!
>   This night
>   Is the thousand and first
>   Ever since love led
>   The one I love close to my heart.
>   To delay the day
>   Its next return
>   Am I not like Allah himself!
>
>   Ever since love led
>   The one I love close to my heart

> This night
> Is the thousand and first.

DINARZADE: But time is fleeting, the hour passes.

THE SULTAN: Yes, indeed,
> Dinarzade is right! Finish, dear lover,
> That story that just yesterday your charming mouth
> Interrupted at its most beautiful moment.

THE SULTANA: So you still like these stories?

THE SULTAN: Yes! No doubt!
> Each morning I listen to them
> With new pleasure

DINARZADE: You must satisfy your desire!

THE SULTAN: Let us listen
> Let us make the most
> Of this moment!
> Start over,
> Finish,
> That novel
> So romantic and charming!

TOGETHER:

THE SULTAN AND DINARZADE	THE SULTANA
Ah! Speak! Speak!	Whatever you want,
The shade still covers	Really, I don't know!
The starry skies	My troubled spirits
Until daybreak	Are still asleep!
Ah! Speak! Speak!	You sadden me!

DINARZADE: Well then, my sister, we're listening to you.

THE SULTANA: I am under orders from Your Highness and I hasten to… (*Turning towards Dinarzade.*) What story are

The Thousand and Second Night

you talking about again?

DINARZADE: (*A bit embarrassed.*) I don't know. For the first time yesterday, I think I fell asleep listening to you.

THE SULTANA: (*Smiling.*) Yes. I noticed. Apparently my stories are no longer interesting to anyone.

THE SULTAN: Don't believe that! Your last one charmed me more than all the others. I didn't miss a single word. This time it's about Leila and the young Corasmin.

THE SULTANA: Ah! Very well. I'll continue, and I beg Your Highness to lend me a most attentive ear. (*After a moment of silence.*) By the way, where did I leave off?

THE SULTAN: Right when the sultan of the Indies catches the young Corasmin at the feet of the princess.

THE SULTANA: Good. I'm there. The sultan of the Indies catches the young Corasmin at Leila's knees…

THE SULTAN: And…?

THE SULTANA: And…it's unique! I don't know anymore….

THE SULTAN: What!

THE SULTANA: May Your Highness please excuse me; my memory fails me.

THE SULTAN: That's impossible!

THE SULTANA: I don't know what I'm feeling! I've tried hard…I can't remember the rest of this tale.

THE SULTAN: Do you jest?

THE SULTANA: No, really!

THE SULTAN: Continue!

DINARZADE: Continue, my sister!

THE SULTANA: Impossible!

THE SULTAN: (*Getting up.*) Well then!

THE SULTANA: Well then, Sire, I'll be frank with you: my imagination exhausted itself in telling so many successive stories for a thousand and one nights; this one was the last one that my memory could store, and I even anticipated that I would probably have to stop in the middle…

THE SULTAN: Really?

THE SULTANA: I beg your majesty's forgiveness.

THE SULTAN: Listen to me! From the day I punished an unworthy sultana who had betrayed her oath of faithfulness to me, I vowed to put to death each morning the new wife that I would choose each night; the first one who placed their feet in this palace came to me resigned to her fate; it was you! Your youth, your spirit, your graceful stories have prolonged your existence up until now, but my vow still holds, and I will have to carry it out the day you remain silent!….

DINARZADE: Oh! My poor sister!

THE SULTAN: Come now, Scheherazade, there is no way that you can't remember the end of this story.

THE SULTANA: I wish I knew it, Sire!

THE SULTAN: Scheherazade, be careful, you make light of me! What did Corasmin do at the princess's feet ….

THE SULTANA: I never knew, but my life is in Your Highness's hands.

THE SULTAN: Woe to you then! Since I made a vow in the name of Allah! Leave me! Leave me! Here comes the day!...

(*The sultana and her sister exit.*)

SCENE III.

THE SULTAN.

THE SULTAN: (*Alone.*) So it's come to her confronting me to my face! She dares to play with my anger! Let's see! Let's calm ourselves down! Scheherazade wants to test my love! She wants to push my patience to the edge! It's a whim! A fantasy!...Well then! We'll see who backs down between the two of us!

(*Hassan enters.*)

SCENE IV.

THE SULTAN, HASSAN.

THE SULTAN: Ah! It's you, Hassan!

HASSAN: I wanted to be the first to greet Your Highness by bringing him the magnificent book, a collection, on his orders, of the sultana's stories.

The Sultan and Scheherazade

THE SULTAN: Hand over that book, Hassan.

(*He opens it and starts skimming it from right to left in the Arabic tradition.*)

Here they are, those tales that enchanted me so! The story of Sinbad the Sailor, the adventures of Haroun al Rachid, Aladdin and his amazing lamp!

HASSAN: Yes, the memory and the imagination of our beloved sultana are inexhaustible.

THE SULTAN: (*Throwing the book away.*) Inexhaustible! What do you know about that you miserable slave? (*He gestures for him to approach.*) Come forward and tell me what brings you here.

HASSAN:	What's got into him? (*Out loud.*) Based on your orders, Sire, everything is in place to celebrate with great pomp and circumstance the thousand and first night of your love…
THE SULTAN:	The thousand and first night!
HASSAN:	Garlands of greenery and exquisite rugs now decorate all the streets of your capital city. (*To himself.*) He seems furious! (*Out loud.*) The road leading to the mosque is lined with fragrant flowers. (*To himself.*) I don't get this change at all. (*Out loud.*) And tonight splendid illuminations will prolong the day well into the night.
THE SULTAN:	Garlands of flowers will soon be replaced with funerary hangings, and all the fires will be extinguished by daybreak, since the sultana will die!
HASSAN:	The sultana!
THE SULTAN:	Listen! You owe me everything, Hassan, you were just a poor slave ripped away from the sands of Arabia when I met you in the streets of Teheran half dead from hunger and cold; I made you my favorite; you must obey me. You'll prepare the sultana's torture, and you'll warn Ermezzin, the executor of my high justice.
HASSAN:	Me!
THE SULTAN:	Do you hear me! You yourself, and in the greatest secrecy.
HASSAN:	That's not possible.
THE SULTAN:	Moreover, you'll look for the young girl who, tonight, will become the sultana who will die tomorrow among the bourgeois, the barons, or merchants.

	Execute my orders carefully or you'll answer with your head.
HASSAN:	I can no longer hold myself up.
THE SULTAN:	The hour of the divan has arrived. I'll meet you back here.

SCENE V.

HASSAN, *alone and then with* THE SULTANA.

HASSAN:	O dire day! The sultana will die! Alas! Dinarzade won't survive such a thing! Dinarzade! My dear Dinarzade!...
THE SULTANA:	Hello, Hassan!
HASSAN:	The sultana!
THE SULTANA:	What were you just thinking of?
HASSAN:	Of defying the sultan's orders.
THE SULTANA:	You know very well that such a thing is impossible!
HASSAN:	And yet I would sacrifice my life in order to have the right to disobey him!
THE SULTANA:	The order he gave you was that terrible then?
HASSAN:	Alas!
THE SULTANA:	The sultan didn't let you chat with those pretty birds that the King of Bengal just sent him!

HASSAN:	It's not that at all!
THE SULTANA:	He forbade you to look at those beautiful porcelain figurines that the King of Japan presented him with.
HASSAN:	I would love it if the sultan had considered me a mere child!
THE SULTANA:	What, he honored you by considering you a man, and you're not proud of that!
HASSAN:	It's not a man he sees in me, but an executioner!
THE SULTANA:	Ah! You're the one he assigned this matter to.
HASSAN:	You call this a matter!
THE SULTANA:	Of this ceremony, if you wish!
HASSAN:	You're breaking my heart! But what on earth did you do? What crime did you commit?
THE SULTANA:	An unforgivable crime! This morning my memory failed me, and I wasn't able to finish my story ….
HASSAN:	That's it?
THE SULTANA:	That's it!
HASSAN:	Well then, with a little imagination…
THE SULTANA:	Everything is marked out in this world, Hassan, even a woman's imagination, and I could bang on my forehead a million times, nothing else can come out of it anymore.
HASSAN:	But perhaps we could help you!

THE SULTANA: No!

HASSAN: Who knows! Is it an extraordinary tale?

THE SULTANA: It's not extraordinary, it's dreadful.

HASSAN: Dreadful!

THE SULTANA: And you yourself would die of fright if you only knew the first words of it!

HASSAN: No matter, my idea is good and I'll persist with it.

THE SULTANA: And then I produced a very simple reasoning about this matter: either the sultan loves me and he'll renounce his fatal oath! Or else he doesn't and there would always be a time when my stories would fail; so he would still talk of putting me to death: it's better to be done with it once and for all today.

HASSAN: But the sultan will be furious with you! And despite all the love you showed him, he won't show you any mercy!

THE SULTANA: Get everything ready for the ceremony then!

HASSAN: It's him!

THE SULTANA: Let's get out of here!

HASSAN: Why don't you at least try to appease him.

THE SULTANA: There's no point. Let him take our place! (*They exit.*)

SCENE VI.

THE SULTAN.

THE SULTAN: (*Alone.*) I'm finally by myself! My head's on fire! … Damned chatterboxes! It seems as though they chose this day to discuss the most unbearable matters! (*He sits down near the table—his hand meets the book Hassan brought him.*) Ah! That book again!... (*He opens it and skims the first few pages.*) When she is no longer here, I'll read them again and think of her, of those wonderful tales she used to cradle my awakenings each morning! …

ROMANCE

Charming tales
What sweet moments
I spent listening to you!
Alas who could give me back
Your sweet moments,
Charming tales!

Your palaces of gold and porphyry
Opened up their enchanted gardens to me!
To your amber and myrrh fragrances
I intoxicated my elated senses!
I wandered through wonderland
On the white feather of death
And your incomparable princesses
Dazzled my astonished eyes

Charming tales
What sweet moments
I spent listening to you!
Alas who could give me back

Your sweet moments,
Charming tales!

With his lively and mocking voice
Sinbad entertained my worries
And with his amazing lamp
Aladdin lit up my nights
Speaking bird, singing tree
No longer had any secrets for me
And I loved the touching story
Of the three Kalendars, sons of sultans!

Charming tales
What sweet moments
I spent listening to you!
Alas who could give me back
Your sweet moments,
Charming tales!

SCENE VII.

THE SULTAN, HASSAN.

HASSAN: Your orders have been carried out!

THE SULTAN: My orders have been carried out?

HASSAN: Yes, Sire.

THE SULTAN: What orders?

HASSAN: The orders that Your Highness gave me.

THE SULTAN: I gave you some orders?

HASSAN: Dreadful ones!

THE SULTAN: Did you choose a merchant's daughter for me?

HASSAN: What daughter?

THE SULTAN: The sultana I asked you to bring to me.

HASSAN: A sultana?

THE SULTAN: Aren't you supposed to lead her into my palace tonight at sundown?

HASSAN: At sundown?

THE SULTAN: (*Impatiently.*) Isn't the sun setting tonight?

HASSAN: It will set no doubt; it has very predictable habits!

THE SULTAN: Well then, what about this sultana?

HASSAN: May Your Highness please forgive me, I combed through the most beautiful neighborhood of your capital city, and I have to admit that the female component of your subjects is quite defective this year.

THE SULTAN: What do you mean by that?

HASSAN: I mean that there is not one among them who is worthy of replacing the sultana Scheherazade; the prettiest one had a shoulder that was higher than the other and her waist was deformed.

THE SULTAN: My subjects are rather audacious in having girls like that!

HASSAN: This came about, Sire, after your union with Scheherazade, they thought that Your Highnesss would no longer give them the honor of choosing a sultana from their families, and so they no longer bothered with it so much!...

THE SULTAN: What is it with everyone today? Even my favorite is making fun of me!

HASSAN: I beg your pardon, Sire, but I have been searching for entire years without being able to provide a worthy replacement for the sultana!

THE SULTAN: Shut up! You're enjoying ripping apart my heart!

HASSAN: Your Highness should have anticipated that this would happen to him! Scheherazade's memory couldn't be inexhaustible.

THE SULTAN: But haven't you figured out that this is pure stubbornness on her part, and that her imagination will allow her not only to finish this bedeviled tale, but also to invent a thousand more if need be!

HASSAN: You think so?

THE SULTAN: I know so!

HASSAN: Well then, Sire, there is a way to get you out of this jam!

THE SULTAN: Speak, Hassan, and my crown jewels, my palaces are all yours.

HASSAN: It's really very simple, if you love the sultana, agree to forgo the end of that story, and she'll start another one!

THE SULTAN: Oh brother! It would be giving in to a nameless whim!

HASSAN:	That story is so important to you?
THE SULTAN:	Not in the least, but being obeyed is.
HASSAN:	And yet, Sire…
THE SULTAN:	She started this story…she'll finish it.
HASSAN:	But what if it were true that she only knows the beginning of it?
THE SULTAN:	That's impossible!
HASSAN:	It is nonetheless, since she swore it to me!
THE SULTAN:	Is that true?
HASSAN:	I can confirm it to Your Highness! Therefore, please deign to agree to…
THE SULTAN:	I don't believe a word of all this.
THE SULTAN:	Listen, and you'll see, if you are not a fool, that she could finish her story in one word.
HASSAN:	Speak! I'm hanging on to your every word…
THE SULTAN:	A sultan generous and brave
HASSAN:	Brave and generous!
THE SULTAN:	Fell in love with a slave
HASSAN:	Fell in love!
THE SULTAN:	Like a fragrance sweet and smooth
HASSAN:	A fragrance of love!

THE SULTAN: They each exhaled their love

HASSAN: They loved each other without expectations!

THE SULTAN:
    You can see from this story
    I was able to remember,
    One word could end it.
    By keeping quiet, I have to believe,
    The sultana wants to prove to me
    That someone can defy me

HASSAN:
    It's a really simple story.
    Why can't her memory
    Finish it off?
    If we are to believe that Scheherazade
    By her silence wants to defy him
    We have to save her.

THE SULTAN: Within the happiness by her side

HASSAN: Within the happiness

THE SULTAN: Once lived a sister young, beautiful and with pride

HASSAN: A young sister

THE SULTAN: A certain disloyal servant eyed

HASSAN: (*Surprised.*) A certain servant

THE SULTAN: In secret held her heart

HASSAN: Held her heart!

THE SULTAN:
    You can see from this story, etc...

HASSAN:
    Ah great god I don't dare believe
    Such a dark betrayal.
    Alas! Does he want to test me?
    He knows my entire story,
    I'm a goner! I must be dreaming!
    How can I save us?

THE SULTAN: The sultan, one day, catches them together. He raises a dagger against them.

HASSAN: I'm trembling!

THE SULTAN: And….

HASSAN: And…

THE SULTAN: We are here
The story is stuck here I fear

THE SULTAN:	HASSAN:
If despite my anger	Mollify your anger
She insists on remaining silent	Hear my prayer
It's time to be done with it	Allow yourself to be moved!
I'll know how to punish her	Ah! I'm afraid of dying
(*To himself.*)	I'm really afraid of dying.
Yes I want to punish her.	

THE SULTAN: I must punish such excessive audacity!

HASSAN: Allah! My blood chills.

THE SULTAN: He who offends me will know his fate! Adieu!

HASSAN: I'm a dead man! Death is my date!

THE SULTAN:	HASSAN:
If despite my anger	Mollify your anger
She insists on remaining silent	Hear my prayer
It's time to be done with it	Allow yourself to be moved!
I'll know how to punish her	Ah! I'm afraid of dying
(*To himself.*)	I'm really afraid of dying.
Yes I want to punish her.	

(*The sultan exits.*)

SCENE VIII.

HASSAN, *alone.*

HASSAN: My story! It's my own story! Oh! My poor Dinarzade! The sultan knows all about our love for each other. We're goners! But how was the sultana able to tell him this story? We're goners!

SCENE IX.

HASSAN, DINARZADE *then* THE SULTANA.

HASSAN: Ah! Dina! My beloved! I'm a dead man!

DINARZADE: You!

HASSAN: The sultan knows everything! He knows of our love.

DINARZADE: Oh Heavens! Who told him?...

THE SULTANA: Me, my sister! Me from whom you hid and who figured everything out, me who unbeknownst to you protected your mysterious trysts more than once.

HASSAN: And Your Majesty told your story to the sultan.

THE SULTANA: Alas! Yes.

DINARZADE: Why?

THE SULTANA: I have to admit that I began this story because I didn't know any other ones, but when I started it I made up my mind never to finish it.

HASSAN: But what he does know is enough for him to understand everything.

THE SULTANA: Don't worry! The adventure was told using hypothetical names and he doesn't know that it was all about you yet!

DINARZADE: What should we be worried about?

HASSAN: What should be hoping for?

THE SULTANA: Above all you should fear that the sultan might find out your secret because if that were the case, all would be lost. Continue to contain your secret loves, and may Allah protect us! Leave me now though as I need to be alone – Go!...

HASSAN: (*To Dinarzade.*) Let's separate.

(*They each go off in separate directions.*)

SCENE X.

THE SULTANA, *alone.*

THE SULTANA: (*Laughing.*) Ah my dear Sultan! You'll end up sparing all my future tales! Allow me to remain silent or kill me!

SCENE XI.

THE SULTANA, THE SULTAN.

THE SULTAN: Scheherazade!

THE SULTANA: Well then! Have you warned the ferocious Ermezzin?

THE SULTAN: You laugh as you ask me that?

THE SULTANA: Come now, dear sultan, I have to come up with a reason. I don't have the right to be angry, if I die tonight it's because I really want to.

THE SULTAN: What?

THE SULTANA: Probably because I started a story I couldn't finish!

THE SULTAN: So why did you choose that one?

THE SULTANA: For a very simple reason! I didn't have any other ones!

THE SULTAN: But that's enough to bang one's head against a wall!

THE SULTANA: If Your Majesty tries that he would be doing it in vain because the walls wouldn't hesitate to be respectful enough to open up for him.

THE SULTAN: You're pushing me to the edge!

THE SULTANA: Summon the ferocious Ermezzin!...

THE SULTAN: Scheherazade! I can't live without you.

THE SULTANA: Come now! You should stay away from such ideas. I want my ... departure to still be an occasion filled with brilliance and splendor for you; I'll be adorned as though I were a young bride dressed in white and crowned with roses; I want the whole court to be brought together for such a splendid celebration and that joyous songs might accompany my last breath all the way to my celestial dwellings.

THE SULTAN: And what I want is that my palace no longer be a giant mausoleum, that cypresses grow in my deserted gardens and that every mosque in the empire ring in songs of suffering.

THE SULTANA: Your Majesty will do no such thing and will respect, I hope, the sultana's last wishes.

SULTAN: But I love you! I love you, Scheherazade.

THE SULTANA: I see that because if you didn't love me you would just let me live, we would spend some more happy days and then satiety would come rather quickly; while this way we will leave each other a bit more promptly, it's true, but I would have kept up until my last hour the absolute certainty of being loved by you. It might be time for the ferocious Ermezzin.

THE SULTAN: No! Be quiet, Scheherazade.

THE SULTANA: You must keep your vow…isn't that right?

THE SULTAN: Undoubtedly! I swore to Allah!

THE SULTANA: Well then, since you swore to Allah! The case is closed! Show some resolve!

THE SULTAN: But, in all honesty, nothing prevents me from sparing you if I wanted to…

THE SULTANA: (*Lively.*) What! You want to…

THE SULTAN: I didn't say that exactly! You need to finish your story first, that damned story, that unfortunate story… which doesn't interest me in the least mind you!

THE SULTANA: What, Your Majesty isn't interested in my stories? That is not very gracious. But, while we're at it, have you picked a new sultana yet?

THE SULTAN: Could there be a woman in the world worthy of succeeding you?

THE SULTANA: It's quite an honor, but in any case quantity will replace quality; besides which for a man who is destined to be a widow every single morning, I suggest you don't attach yourself to any woman at all!

THE SULTAN: Ah, I'll swear to that…

THE SULTANA: If I were you, I would give up this habit of swearing once and for all! An oath is quickly forgotten and it doesn't take long before we regret it!

THE SULTAN: Oh yes! An oath is a terrible thing!

THE SULTANA: After that, your own was made during a moment of legitimate anger and up until a certain point it gave you a high probability of never being cheated on again.

THE SULTAN: What do you mean by "up until a certain point"?

THE SULTANA: No doubt! But what is this certainty of faithfulness from a wife who doesn't have time to be unfaithful? And what about the lovely pleasure of giving one's heart to women who only have twelve hours to live and whose kisses are already chilled by the cold from the grave! Won't you summon the ferocious Ermezzin for me!

THE SULTAN: Oh, Scheherazade! More, more, a few moments more!

THE SULTANA: So let's talk about cheerier things! You look like a sultan in despair, and you'll wind up imparting some sad thoughts onto me, like the will to live. And here! A chess game!

THE SULTAN: Me? Play at such a time!

DUO

THE SULTANA: Come on now, Master
Do come around to my prayer
This game will be the last
You should be the victor.

THE SULTAN: Of my happiness,
This hour will be its last?
Terror follows anger,
Alas, I'm afraid.

(*Sitting down on the table.*)

If only I weren't the sultan!

THE SULTANA: Play, I'm waiting for you!

THE SULTAN: If only I weren't the sultan
I would say: let's run off together
Let's leave this place for good.
That a same hope should bring us together!
Let's flee with all our love!

THE SULTANA: If only you weren't the sultan!

THE SULTAN: Speak, I'm listening to you!

THE SULTANA: If only you weren't the sultan
          I would tell you: Master, where does one throw
          your horseman?
          Your soldiers are losing their heads!
          Your madmen are mad as hatters!
          (*Playing.*)
          Check for the queen

THE SULTAN: I would save her!
          Or I would perish!

THE SULTANA: The king is defending his queen!

THE SULTAN: Yes, I have no fear for myself!

THE SULTANA: In that case, check for the king!
          And to finish the battle
          Checkmate.

TOGETHER:
THE SULTAN: THE SULTANA:
  Of my happiness,   For you, master,
  This hour will be its last?   This defeat will be your last,
  Terror follows anger,   From now on you will be, I hope
  Alas, I'm afraid.   Forever the victor.

THE SULTANA: Yet victory annoys you
              And intensifies your worries!

THE SULTAN: Of the trouble that now agitates me
              What do you gain from laughing at me so?

THE SULTANA: (*She picks up a guzla.*[1]) A song might please you
              more no doubt!

---

1. A guzla is a single stringed instrument traditionally used in the Dinarides region and Serbia played with a bow. Prosper Mérimée wrote a book of short stories called *The Guzla* (*La Guzla*, 1827), a book of tales from Central Europe filled with gothic horror elements such as vampires and other creatures.

THE SULTAN: A song!

THE SULTANA: Are you listening to me?

THE SULTAN: (*Despondently.*) I'm listening!

THE SULTANA: Why is it that in the Persian Gulf
There so many boats with triple masts?
Why should it be that in the Arabian sands
One should go from Medina to Damascus?
Flee, Sailors, both the Grecian seas
And shores unknown!
Don't stray too far from Mecca.
Pious pilgrims with bare feet!

Love is the supreme law
From Allah who created days,
Love, love the one who loves you
Love is the only happiness there is.

What's the point of crossing the Caucasus
Soldiers, for far away battles?
Your crown is crushing you,
Kings who give orders from down here.
Leave them in peace in their own kingdoms
The Arabs and the Muslims.
And choose a thatched roof over
The sultan's golden throne.
Love is the supreme law
From Allah who created days,
Love, love the one who loves you
Love is the only happiness there is.

THE SULTAN: Love is the only happiness there is.

THE SULTAN:	THE SULTANA:
O my beloved,	Yes, I was loved!
Don't leave me!	But your soul, alas,

> My existence is surrounded
> By worries down here!
> Stay, out of pity!
> Can I live without you?
> If you don't want me to die
> Stay by my side!
> To indulgence is now closed!
> Don't accuse me!
> Despite myself, I'm crying
> I yield to the law
> That demands that I die.
> You'll live without me

THE SULTANA: The fatal hour approaches!

THE SULTAN: Just one more moment together!

THE SULTANA: No, think about your oath!

THE SULTAN: I can't save you without perjuring myself.

THE SULTANA: What are you saying?

THE SULTAN: If you finish your story, I swear, in return
To never expose you to any such adventures any more.
Speak! Yield to my wishes, and regain on this day
Both my strength and my love

THE SULTANA: But no! It's impossible
I've tried so hard to find…

THE SULTAN: Well then?

THE SULTANA: I can't find a thing
Adieu! Stop hesitating and become inflexible!

TOGETHER:

THE SULTAN:	THE SULTANA:
O my beloved,	Yes, I was loved!
Don't leave me!	But your soul, alas,
My existence is surrounded	To indulgence is now closed!
By worries down here!	Don't accuse me!
Stay, out of pity!	Despite myself, I'm crying

Can I live without you?	I yield to the law
If you don't want me to die	That demands that I die.
Stay by my side!	You'll live without me

(*As the sultana exits she blows one last kiss to the sultan.*)

SCENE XII.

THE SULTAN, *alone.*

THE SULTAN: Come now! No more weakness! No more pity! You must! But who's that coming this way? Hassan and Dizarzade! They're accusing me of cruelty no doubt! They're conspiring against me in order to save the sultana. Let's listen! (*He hides behind the tapestry that closes the right-hand door.*)

SCENE XIII.

HASSAN, DINARZADE.

HASSAN: Listen my poor Dina, we have to cough everything up to the sultan. It's the only way we can save Scheherazade!

DINARZADE: What's that again?

HASSAN: When he finds out that the story she refuses to complete is our own, he might forgive her silence, and all of his anger will fall on my shoulders alone…

DINARZADE: Your shoulders alone?

HASSAN: Yes! I'll die happy if my death can save the both of you.

DINARZADE: Be quiet! Be quiet!

HASSAN:
    1
At your feet that I adore
Before fleeing the dawn
I want to recite to you once more
Our sweet love vows.
As never will my tenderness
Abandon you.
Farewell, dear mistress
Oh my Dina!

    2
Pour that flame again
Into my enchanted heart!
All the way to the bottom of my soul
Pour the voluptuousness
And that supreme charm
That fascinated me
Farewell, everything that I love,
Oh my Dina!

    3
By this ardor that intoxicates me
I feel myself consumed.
I'll stop living
Without stopping my love for you.
As my delighted soul
Gave itself entirely to you!
Farewell, my entire life
Oh my Dina!

DINARZADE: Hassan, my dear Hassan!

(*She falls into Hassan's arms.*)

HASSAN: The sultan!

SCENE XIV.

HASSAN, DINARZADE, THE SULTAN, PALACE GUARDS.

THE SULTAN: Grab these two guilty ones and take them away!

HASSAN: Spare her!

DINARZADE: Mercy!

THE SULTAN: Obey.

(*They are taken away.*)

THE SULTAN: I understand everything! They were playing tricks on me; they colluded in order to dupe me! The sultana was their accomplice. Ah! She didn't know how the tale would end! Well then, by Allah, I'll provide her with an ending!

SCENE XV.

THE SULTAN, THE COURT, *then* THE SULTANA

THE FINALE

THE CHORUS: Honor! Honor to the great sultan
Of Persia and Hindoustan!
To celebrate her Highness the entire court
Is here.

> Ceaselessly watching over his loves he does deign to do Allah!
>
> Honor! Honor to the great sultan
> Of Persia and Hindoustan!
> To the sultana on this beautiful day
> We must as is the custom
> In order to better prove our love to her
> All pay tribute!
>
> Honor! Honor to the great sultan
> Of Persia and Hindoustan!

THE SULTAN: Cease your festive songs,
Of joy and pleasure.
We are about to go through hell,
The sultana will perish!

THE CHORUS: The sultana will perish!

THE SULTANA: (*She enters all adorned.*)
Here I am all adorned!
I can make my entrance
In the kingdom of the blue god!
Farewell, my dear sultan, farewell!

THE SULTAN: You still refuse to speak?

THE SULTANA: But no doubt
And yet, I'll die from it!

THE SULTAN: In that case, everyone listen to me.
As I know this tale, and I will finish it myself!
Yes, the heroes of this adventure
Were based on real ones!
And I just caught them a few moments ago
In this very place!

Scheherazade

THE SULTANA: What's he saying –Ah! Great Gods!
(*To the sultan.*)
Mercy!

THE SULTAN: Out of the question!

THE SULTANA: Mercy for my sister, for Hassan!
You kill them, heartless, insensitive barbarian,
And you stain my stories with blood!

THE CHORUS: Mercy for her sister, for Hassan!

THE SULTAN: No, I will get revenge my way
              You deserve to learn a lesson!...

THE SULTANA: Pity for the both of them!

THE SULTAN: I will enjoy the glory
              Of finishing your story without you.

THE SULTANA: Alas! Why don't you finally explain yourself!

THE SULTAN: The ending of this novel is unknown to you
              Because in my justified rage
              In order to avenge my outrage,
              To punish them I want for them to be taken
              In the same chains to be shaken
              (*Laughing.*)
              At the Mosque where they have just been wed!

THE SULTANA: They have just been wed!

THE SULTAN: Here they are!

THE CHORUS: Here they are!

THE SULTANA: Oh my God thank you from afar!

SCENE XVI.

THE SAME, HASSAN, DINARZADE

DINARZADE: My sister!

THE SULTAN: The story is now completed!
(*To the sultana.*)
What do you think about the ending?

THE SULTANA: It's charming!

ALL: It's charming!

THE SULTAN: By your songs, my friends, let's celebrate this day!
Allah has freed me from my fatal vow!
(*To the sultana.*)
You are no longer condemned to tremble by my side
I'll give you back with no returns
All my love that burns

DINARZADE *and* HASSAN: To you all of my love that burns!

THE CHORUS: Honor! Honor to the great sultan
Of Persia and Hindoustan!

The End

La Guimard

CAST OF CHARACTERS:

DAVID, a painter.
LA GUIMARD.
VALENTINE.
RÉMY SIRÉSOL, a ballet teacher, 50 years old.
MONSIEUR DE VERGY, 40 years old and fat.
MONSIEUR D'ABRECOURT, 45 years old.
CHANDAS.
A POLICE LIEUTENANT.

The action takes place in Paris, during Louis XVI's reign.

ACT I

The stage represents a painter's studio with a rather mediocre look to it. Canvasses are stuck to the wall; a big painting turns its back to the audience; an easel supports a half-finished portrait of a woman. Straw chairs; on the right, in the background, a door; behind that, a French door leading towards an office – with a door at the end of it.

SCENE I.

DAVID, VALENTINE.

(David is busy modifying the portrait of a woman on the easel. Valentine wanders around him incessantly.)

VALENTINE: Are you almost finished, my dear love?

DAVID: My poor Valentine, I've just started to work.

VALENTINE: For example! You've been staring at that portrait for a long half an hour!

DAVID: A half an hour! That's not much in the scheme of things.

VALENTINE: Too bad if this half an hour went by like five minutes for you! I know half hours that can last several days!

DAVID: You obviously really like me, my sweet!

VALENTINE: Why do you say that?

DAVID: You're asking me why? That's a "why" that sure contradicts my last words! I rule in favor of it!

Jacques-Louis David.

VALENTINE: (*Laughing.*) I'm at your beck and call, *monsieur*; I would still rather fight rather than see you caress that woman's face of yours over there!

DAVID: Jealous child! The only time I touch it is from the tips of my paint brushes!

VALENTINE: Ah! You're going overboard, my friend; since your brushes contain all your talent; and your talent is your entire soul! And your love….

DAVID: (*Getting up.*) Well then, my love is of an overseas color at the moment! – Crazy as you are; here is your dear jealousy which is about to land on the edge of my palette like a bird! I guess you've forgotten that my brain is far from my head, and, while the former delights in the sacred fire that animates this insensitive canvas to the core, in the latter, your beloved image is illuminated by its chaste clarity like a Madonna from the divine Raphael; look into my heart my beloved and you'll see yourself reflected, as genius has held the paint brushes of my love!

VALENTINE: How handsome you are, and how I love you my David.

DAVID: So why are you jealous of this portrait then?

VALENTINE: It's because it's usurped all your attention!

DAVID: Really! I fear one thing however, that it won't be different from its model and that your adored traits, *madame*, might slip through my loving fingers!

VALENTINE: Ah! But that lady and I don't resemble each other in the least; she is pretty, very pretty; and even a bit too pretty.

DAVID: You obviously don't love it?

VALENTINE: Very little!

DAVID: Not at all!

VALENTINE: I'm barely of this world, but her traits and demeanor have a *je ne sais quoi* of determination! Modesty is not brave and that lady seems quite up to the task.

DAVID: My dear Valentine is a bit cowardly!

VALENTINE: And yet you don't frighten me!

DAVID: For example!

VALENTINE: Look at me! – Look at me face to face!

DAVID: (*Not moving.*) I see you!

VALENTINE: Turn around a bit more! – More! – More!

DAVID: Tell me right away that you want me to kiss you.

VALENTINE: No!

DAVID: Or else I'll stop painting!

VALENTINE: That's sort of the point!

DAVID: Jealous one! Fie!

VALENTINE: Come now, my friend! Who is this lady?

DAVID: (*Embarrassed.*) I'm not really sure – I see her a powerful woman! – She'll protect us!

VALENTINE: Too bad!

DAVID: Too bad! As it would be better to walk alone, and not attach oneself to the borders of protection, but the time that envelops us with its shameful speculation is gruesome! What talent wouldn't be stifled under the bramble of injustices and venalities! We have to lean on these haughty oak trees then that lightening will strike down one day! Too bad, my beloved; but it's all for the best if a good hand comes out and plucks us from the crowd, and lifts us all the way up to inaccessible heights; let those great personalities sprinkle their good deeds here and there!

	As they'll soon appreciate that gratitude will soon grow in our hearts!
VALENTINE:	Always your lofty thoughts! Your noble dreams!
DAVID:	Always! They keep me going in my ongoing struggles against nepotism!
VALENTINE:	Well then! And what about my love?
DAVID:	And your love as well, my beloved, your love that will never abandon me; your love, my love, yours and mine, all four of us will go to Rome! Oh! Rome!
VALENTINE:	Good! Don't get sad! And make sure you send your great painting to the competition![1]
DAVID:	(*Turning around.*) There it is leaning so sadly against the wall and turning its back against its author; it tells me that I'm unworthy to have made it, since I'm incapable of producing it in the light of day!
VALENTINE:	My dear David, you'll have to take your courage with both hands and personally call on the members of the jury! You've neglected all your acquaintances, and there isn't a single one of them who can recognize you now! You already won second prize three years ago, it's a good sign that…
DAVID:	I've already submitted my work to four competitions! The second one was favorable, that's true, but the three others publicly noted a distinct lack of artistic merit!

---

1. Patrick Berthier's introduction to the play in Verne's *Théâtre inédit* notes: "They aren't talking about the portrait of la Guimard that David did but rather the gigantic painting *The Loves of Antochius and Stratonice* that will win David the Prix de Rome in 1775." Berthier in Verne's *Théâtre inédit, op.cit.*, 577.

VALENTINE: You're a great, a noble artist, my friend and your discouragement is blasphemy!

DAVID: What have I succeeded in doing since I decided to devote my time and my life to this passion that carries me away!

VALENTINE: You've succeeded in gaining the respect of your friends! And that's not the worst reward for all your work to hear yourself being applauded by those hands that you can shake without shame!

DAVID: (*Talking to himself.*) Why have the beauties of nature impressed themselves on my spirit if I am unable to reproduce them! Why do the lofty accomplishments from antiquity ravage my entire soul, if my hand can't retrace them for modern eyes in order to resurrect the heroes of ancient times after two thousand years of obscurity! Alas! Accomplishing nothing, only making it half way, seeing one's happier competitors trample all over your body, remaining buried among these corpses that pave the road to glory! Is this happiness, is this serenity! Is this life? Well, no it isn't! Here it is! Painting these portraits, and getting paid for them at the highest price possible! – Destiny!

VALENTINE: For you, my friend, I left my guardian's house, I fled the gloomy prospects of an unhappy marriage; before the prejudices of the world, and the laws of morality, I consulted my love; and to answer yours, I made of my passion the consolation for your worries, and of my humble life the servant to your desires! In you, I love your beautiful talent, and your big heart, but far from burdening you with a selfish love, I subject my disinterested driving force to the requirements of your glory! My family is rich and powerful; they enjoy an invincible credit that you could have no doubt profited from! Must my separation from them and my presence here throw you not only into the throes of an upcoming misery, but deprive you of guaranteed protection! Forgive me, dear friend, if all your suffering comes from me! – But I love you; I'll work; I'll use what strength I have, I'll help you with all my soul, I'll encourage you with all my heart, but I love you!

DAVID: Valentine! Valentine! Valentine! You've shared in my worries, you'll share my glory! And I'll have some, even it's just to prove my gratitude! And you'll forgive me for returning such little happiness in exchange for your devotion, since my fame will never attain the heights of your love!

VALENTINE: My poor lover!

DAVID: Come now! A little joy, my sweet! You'll make me cry in my palette and it will no longer be an oil painting!

VALENTINE: Meanie! You're going to send your painting?

DAVID: To the devil!

VALENTINE: No! To the competition! You'll call on the necessary people.

DAVID: I'll be a sad figure.

VALENTINE: In return, I'll prepare your palette.

DAVID: Make sure you put in a bit of your cheeks, eh, it will help me to paint some peaches!

VALENTINE: (*Putting a veil over herself with a handkerchief.*) Meanie!

DAVID: Take that handkerchief away from my sun! I want to paint with a ray from your eyes!

VALENTINE: That's good! That's good! Make sure you don't make that lady look too real!

DAVID: Lunatic!

VALENTINE: You've worked enough on her eyes! Why don't you leave her eyelashes alone! You're making eyes that look straight ahead!

DAVID: Do you want them to be cross-eyed?

VALENTINE: That's it! Adjust the nose! – I yield the nose to you! I'm not jealous of the nose! Ah! Meanie! Could you just not caress that mouth so much! You're giving her lips that are too tender, and I would wager that this painting gives you a kiss when I'm not here!

DAVID: (*Moving towards her.*) In that case! Since you're here…

VALENTINE: Someone! – I'm leaving!

(*She exits to the right of the stage.*)

DAVID: Poor Valentine! What will I become without her?

SCENE II.

DAVID, ABRECOURT, CHANDAS.

ABRECOURT: (*To Chandas; they both stop in front of the door.*) Monsieur the Marquis, if you are the first one to enter this door ….

CHANDAS: Monsieur the Duke, if you are the first one in this room…

ABRECOURT: You'll have some explaining to do!

CHANDAS: You'll have to answer to me!

DAVID: Gentlemen, please!

ABRECOURT: (*To Chandas.*) One step further, sir, and it's a done deal!

CHANDAS: One move, and I draw my pistol!

DAVID: (*To himself.*) Ah all of this! Where are they up to? (*Out loud.*) Is it your pleasure to come in or to go out!

ABRECOURT AND CHANDAS: (*Together.*) Sir, we are in love with the famous Guimard ….

(*They stumble in knocking each other over.*)

ABRECOURT: And you will notice that I was the first one to introduce myself at the door.

CHANDAS: That's an undignified lie!

ABRECOURT: Undignified! You'll retract that!

CHANDAS: Not at all. You better believe it! I arrived before you and I'm holding on to my rights.

ABRECOURT: Your rights! Do you remember that lovely punch I threw you right into your shoulders?

CHANDAS: And that admirable boot that I provided you with in the middle of your leg!

ABRECOURT: Well then, Marquis, let's get on with it. Ah, you have your rights!

(*They both draw their pistols.*)

CHANDAS: I'll sting yours a little bit!

DAVID: (*Screaming more loudly than them.*) Gentlemen, would you please shut up! Do you take my studio for an armory! Who do you think you are!

CHANDAS, ABRECOURT: (*Together.*) I am Chandas, the marquis. I am the Duke of Abrecourt!

DAVID: If you continue like this, there will be no point in pursuing anything further! You both have the same thing to say!

TOGETHER: Yes!

DAVID: Then you might as well take turns telling me everything!

BOTH OF THEM: I'll start! I'll have you know that…

DAVID: Enough! You'll each just speak for a minute!

CHANDAS: I'll start!

ABRECOURT: I'm the one, please!

CHANDAS: Duke!

ABRECOURT: Marquis!

DAVID: Quiet! The one who doesn't start will finish! Go on! (*They are both silent.*) Go on! Speak! Gentlemen! Nothing! I'm handing it over to you!

CHANDAS: Sir, I'm in love with ….

DAVID: In order to save on conversation expenses, please speak in the plural!

CHANDAS: We are in love with the famous Guimard, which is hardly surprising since she's the most beautiful dancer in modern times! We are thought of just as highly and it's thanks to our efforts ….

DAVID: (*To Abrecourt.*) Your turn!

ABRECOURT: Our efforts that she chose you as her ordinary painter…

DAVID: (*Sternly.*) Monsieur the Duke! (*To Chandas.*) Your turn!

CHANDAS: We haven't yet conquered the virtue of our beautiful mistress and for several days now, she has been spurning us, to the point of her slamming her door on us!

DAVID: (*To Abricourt.*) Your turn!

ABRICOURT: And yet, we've vowed to see her at all costs, and we met outside your door, at the exact same time that we both decided to put that plan into action.

DAVID: And so! Why should I care? (*To Chandas.*) Your turn!

CHANDAS: Yet, she is scheduled for a sitting in a half an hour or so; and in order for us to show our appreciation for the care you've shown us in thinking of us, we beg you to hid us in some corner where we can watch her!

DAVID:	So you really like her!
TOGETHER:	We are dying of love for her, and…
DAVID:	Shush! (*To Abrecourt.*) Your turn!
ABRECOURT:	Our rivalry has already earned us the advantage of our having dueled against each other for her twelve times already.
DAVID:	Gentlemen, you must both be full of holes rather than full of fire!
CHANDAS:	We have a bit of credit at the court, and you would know all too well how to abuse it!
ABRECOURT:	You are a painter with much talent, sir, and you will hide us somewhere.
CHANDAS:	Look, here's the portrait of our beautiful beloved.
ABRECOURT:	Ah! There she is!
CHANDAS:	(*To David.*) Make her beautiful, sir, don't hold back on using your brushes.
ABRECOURT:	Make sure you don't skimp on color! Emphasize it. Good.
CHANDAS:	Especially her face, her neck, her shoulders!
ABRICOURT:	And the surrounding areas!
DAVID:	Gentleman, I know what I'm doing; I'm making her foot smaller than her hands!
ABRECOURT:	Oh! I want her hands to be smaller than her mouth.

CHANDAS: As long as her mouth is smaller than her eyes!

DAVID: You will be satisfied! As for hiding you, gentlemen, use this cabinet; but it can only hold one person. I'll be back in a half an hour.

(*The two suitors look at each other with devouring eyes.*)

CHANDAS: (*To the duke.*) I think you easily understand that I will not give up my place for you!

ABRECOURT: Nor shall I, Marquis!

CHANDAS: Since I got here first, I have the right…

ABRECOURT: To leave as well!

DAVID: They're starting again!

CHANDAS: Duke, don't get my ears all heated up.

ABRECOURT: I'll cut them off, that's all!

CHANDAS: You'll cut this conversation short; that's all you'll be cutting!

ABRECOURT: Me give up! Pox to you!

CHANDAS: Duke, this is a duel to the death!

ABRECOURT: One of us will be left on the ground.

DAVID: (*To himself.*) It continues! I'm getting out of here!

SCENE III.

ABRECOURT, CHANDAS.

(*They are becoming more and more animated.*)

CHANDAS:	Do you know that the other day la Guimard gave me uncontestable proof that she preferred me to you! And she put her hand on my shoulder!
ABRECOURT:	To you!
CHANDAS:	To me!
ABRECOURT:	She was in a rush; she stumbled on you on her way somewhere, she vigorously pushed you to the point where you lost your balance! – That's all.
CHANDAS:	Horrors!
ABRECOURT:	Meanwhile, a while ago, she leaned against my arm.
CHANDAS:	Because she lost her footing and she was about to fall!
ABRECOURT:	Infamy!
CHANDAS:	We have equal rights to her then, and there is one of us too many in this world!
ABRECOURT:	Let's take this outside then!
CHANDAS:	*En garde!*
ABRECOURT:	*En garde!*

(*They go off to fight each other.*)

SCENE IV.

ABRECOURT, CHANDAS, LA GUIMARD, RÉMY.

RÉMY: (*Stuttering.*) A duel-el!

LA GUIMARD: A duel! Rémy! Break them up!

RÉMY: May the heavens-ns protect me! All-all they have-have to do is pierce-ce m-my calf-ff!

LA GUIMARD: Rémy! Gentlemen!

(*The fighters stop fighting.*)

RÉMY: (*Laughing.*) Those two again!

LA GUIMARD: Always those two!

CHANDAS, ABRECOURT: Beautiful Guimard, please believe that...

LA GUIMARD: Be quiet! What are you doing here?

RÉMY: Yes-sss. What are you doing here?

CHANDAS, ABRECOURT: We bumped into each other by accident.

RÉMY: Gentlemennnn in loooovvvvve, with your passing loooovvvvve affairs, you tur-urn your heads towards my be-be-you-tiful student, and me-ee, Rémy-ii Sirésol, her dance teacher, I order you to take your legs to your necks!

LA GUIMARD: Well then! Are you listening?

CHANDAS: We've come to admire your portrait.

ABRECOURT: Your beautiful portrait.

CHANDAS: Your superb portrait.

ABRECOURT: Your magnificent portrait.

CHANDAS: Your sublime portrait…

ABRECOURT: (*Searching.*) Your ....

La Guimard

LA GUIMARD: (*Laughing.*) Ha! Ha! Ha!

RÉMY: One, two! Nobody say a thing! Your sublime portrait! Who can top that?

ABRECOURT: (*Searching.*) Your ….

RÉMY: Three! Your sublime portrait! Sold to the Marquis of Chandas!

CHANDAS: So this cabinet belongs to me!

ABRECOURT: For example!

RÉMY: So that's why they're fighting!

LA GUIMARD: You're still following me! You're still spying on me. Your presence offends me, you bore me with your attentions, you assault me with compliments, and yet you still come over here and start again even at other people's places! Your duels haven't tired of the Bois de Boulogne, or the Porte Maillot; they've come here to bloody my painter's studio and I see that you're ready to impale each other just for a cabinet! Zounds, I'm arrogating the right to decide for you and in order to please you both, stop quarreling and start walking out!

RÉMY: Wel-ll said! Very well-ll said.

ABRECOURT: But ….

LA GUIMARD: But as far as I'm concerned it's irrelevant whether you pierce yourselves or not in what you have at heart under the clothes, as long as your cries don't pierce my ears! Go on, hit the road!

CHANDAS, ABRECOURT: (*To themselves.*) I'm sticking around.

(*They exit.*)

SCENE V.

LA GUIMARD, RÉMY.

LA GUIMARD: Those nuisances – those fools – they've left!

RÉMY: You treat them harshly my dear student!

LA GUIMARD: You see, old bean, those two admirers' protests do harm to my nerves.

RÉMY: And to your muscles as well, as the hollow of your knee isn't giving me anything anymore! Moreover, when love comes so easily to you, why would you want to make it insurmountable?

LA GUIMARD: Insurmountable! Did you say insurmountable! Fine! We'll see!

RÉMY: While we wait, I composed a new step and yet you don't want to learn it!

LA GUIMARD: I have lots of time! My head is filled with complicated things.

RÉMY: And your heart?

LA GUIMARD: My heart! What are you talking about? Didn't you see a bit of my heart at the Opera? If men only found heart underneath, they would soon have enough of it!

RÉMY: And yet, you love your painter.

LA GUIMARD: Yes! In my own way! When I noticed that he wasn't paying attention to me, my feelings were hurt; when I saw that he was paying attention to someone else, I became jealous; all these scrambled and mixed-up feelings as a result of my capriciousness, and my stubbornness!

RÉMY: But why did you come a half an hour before your sitting! – Only your damned painter isn't here!

LA GUIMARD: Good!

RÉMY: Why?

LA GUIMARD: So you don't know anything then, you don't see anything then, you don't understand anything then! – What are you good for?

RÉMY: Zounds, I'm still balancing a *balancé* correctly, and I'm nobly cobbling an *entrechat* step!

LA GUIMARD: And after that!

RÉMY: After that! There's an after? That's it. What more can one do in a minuet?

LA GUIMARD: You don't know what love is do you?

RÉMY: True love, is a very slow minuet, very formal with *force* salutations, *force* bows;[2] you take his hand, and you get married, to the third reverence – at the Opera, you just don't take time to do it; crack! You've just invented the conjugal *entrechat*! In two minutes you've finished a sentimental *gavotte* and all day, you are immersed in dance.

---

2. He is using ballet jargon to describe love and courtship.

Sophie Arnould.

LA GUIMARD: In that case, love is not very likely!

RÉMY: Yes, in an hour! ... Just a short interval between one whim and another.

LA GUIMARD: In any case! Whim or no whim, David will be my lover!

RÉMY: I'm not contradicting you! What surprises me is that he isn't yet, because ….

LA GUIMARD: Because it's been eight long days that I've been coming, hasn't it! My portrait is coming along, and my affaires are not! Destiny! There's always a dumb hussy spinning around him, and I've had trouble getting a minute of face-to-face time in there edgewise!

RÉMY: What you really want is for him not to be involved with that little girl!

LA GUIMARD: And who the hell knows what kind of little girl it is, a cousin, a sister, a servant, an anything; but I imagine that she loves him, that David, since jealousy comes out of all her pores when she sees me!

RÉMY: Brava, my dear student, brava for your rivalry; come! Look! Win: but whatever you do in the name of heaven, dance! Don't give up this amazing talent that nature and I have engrained in you, this talent that will bring the great princes of the earth to your knees; love your David, for an hour, for an entire day if you'd like, but not more than that.

LA GUIMARD: I feel like I'm going to love him for eight days!

RÉMY: I'm opposed to that!

LA GUIMARD: My little Rémy, you'll dance what you'll want to dance, but I'll love him for eight days! Four days to depress his sweetie, and four days just for me; come on now, I'm not asking for too much am I!

RÉMY: You are in fact! You've already sent your most powerful admirers packing and you've neglected to do your ballet exercises; you can no longer stand on the tips of your fingers; here, have a look! (*He stands on his tip-toes.*) There was a time when you could dance

	on your nails; take care to make it to one step below Sophie Arnould's level.[3]
LA GUIMARD:	Her! – A woman who dances from her shoulders and who does *entrechats* accompanied by the sound of her own bones!
RÉMY:	Agreed.
LA GUIMARD:	Go ahead, old bean, go ask my fans whose pirouettes they prefer, mine or hers!!
RÉMY:	Yes! But your fans will abandon you, and the most powerful among them will bow out!
LA GUIMARD:	Let's go then! I need to.
RÉMY:	Why?
LA GUIMARD:	Because my painter, David, has made a beautiful painting that, without me, won't be accepted into the competition, but through high connections, I'll be able to have him crowned with success!
RÉMY:	But it's worthless.
LA GUIMARD:	Come now! We have talent, and we'll see if glory and seduction will triumph over the loves of virgins whose reality is no more amusing than a dream would be! Am I not worth more than that little girl?
RÉMY:	Not at all! Excuse me! You're worth a hundred times more; I'm sure the hollow of her knee is not made of iron.

---

[3]. Sophie Anould (1744-1802) was actually a great singer at the time. She was known not only for her great talent but for her nasty tongue especially against competitors. Berthier mentions that she even criticized la Guimard for being too skinny (Berthier in Verne's *Théâtre inédit, op.cit.*, 588).

LA GUIMARD: Nor an incendiary demeanor!

RÉMY: Nor an adorable kick!

LA GUIMARD: Nor impossible eyes! – You can see that I'll have that David; but I have to see him face to face; and the end of the portrait is almost finished!

RÉMY: With all that, your portrait is rather pretty.

LA GUIMARD: What do you mean by that?

RÉMY: A dancer that doesn't feature her feet in a portrait; but what good is it to have such features if you let yourself be cut in half by the frame! Isn't that the essence of female beauty, my lovely! Great Scott, I would rather have myself painted from my feet up to and including my knees, I swear that people would recognize them right away!

LA GUIMARD: Lunatic!

RÉMY: You have a pretty face; I think I've never noticed that before! – Let's have a look? Yes! Not bad; but you don't know your feet, my girl; your eyes are big, and your hair; but blazes, you can't dance on your head!

LA GUIMARD: Were you planning on sharing your observations with David – then he'll be all mine! And when I will have sunk the little girl?

RÉMY: How brazen of you! – But what if she doesn't leave him?

LA GUIMARD: Hey, idiot, I came early so that I could be alone with him! – When he comes back, I'll pick him up and it'll be just the two of us from now on! – Do me a favor and go compose some steps by the door. (*She turns around.*) Someone's there! It's him!

SCENE VI.

LA GUIMARD, RÉMY, VERGY.

RÉMY: It's not him!

VERGY: You, *Madame*.

LA GUIMARD: You, *Monsieur*.

VERGY: My former beloved.

LA GUIMARD: My former admirer.

VERGY: Ah! How about that, you were abducted, weren't you?

LA GUIMARD: Who do you think I am?

RÉMY: Yes! Who do you think we are? You ought to know that we've already been abducted several times and you won't get any cut from them!

VERGY: Ah! How about that; nothing escapes this Jupiter, does it; proper young girls and dancers ....

LA GUIMARD: And ....

RÉMY: Yes, and the ....

LA GUIMARD: And the…come on, hurry up! What are you doing here?

VERGY: (*Handing her a letter.*) Are you familiar with this?

LA GUIMARD: A signet letter.[4]

VERGY: A bit!

LA GUIMARD: Ah, that! Whose place do you think you're in?

VERGY: I don't think, I'm sure that I'm at David the painter's.

LA GUIMARD: And you obtained that letter against him!

VERGY: I can boast of it!

LA GUIMARD: So you're all powerful!

VERGY: You can judge for yourself! I have friends in high places, I am and I obtain everything I want! To get revenge on the painter, I made myself the new jury chair of the Institute, and in order to send him to prison, I obtained this order! That way I'll be able to punish both him and his glory!

LA GUIMARD: What if he puts on an exhibit?

VERGY: I'll turn him down!

LA GUIMARD: And if you find him?

VERGY: I'll lock him up!

LA GUIMARD: What did he ever do to you?

VERGY: What did he do! Right when I was about to marry my ward off to my nephew, he abducted her!

---

4. A *lettre de cachet* was a letter from the King containing direct orders that could not be questioned (usually involving the arrest and imprisonment of a subject).

LA GUIMARD: Your ward.

RÉMY: She just made a *faux pas*! – That's what happens when you don't know how to dance! At least, in the ballet corpus, we do make *faux pas*; but we always land on our legs.

VERGY: And then?

RÉMY: And then nothing! That's it!

LA GUIMARD: So that's your ward I see constantly attached to that David?

VERGY: Attached?

RÉMY: Attached – hung! Hung is the right word! A man's triumph is to look like the gallows!

VERGY: And then!

RÉMY: And then!

LA GUIMARD: Shush! – And do you think that your ward loves this painter?

VERGY: Love indeed, since she turned down my nephew!

RÉMY: Maybe your nephew is horrible!

VERGY: I am his uncle, sir.

LA GUIMARD: And what do you intend to do?

VERGY: It's very simple: I'm going to throw him in the Bastille!

LA GUIMARD: Do you know him?

VERGY: Not in the least! But by reputation. He's one of those people who practices true love, that kind of love that begins with an abduction and ends in a suicide. This David is a knight from the Middle Ages who wears his lady's colors and devotes his entire life to her service! There's no chance that another woman might triumph instead and the most unbelievable seductions would have no effect on his heart!

LA GUIMARD: Is that what you think?

VERGY: I'm sure of it!

RÉMY: (*To la Guimard.*) Why don't we take off, how about that!

LA GUIMARD: Why?

RÉMY: There's nothing left for us to do here!

VERGY: What brings you to this painter's place?

RÉMY: We're not here by accident.

VERGY: (*To la Guimard.*) Do you know him?

RÉMY: We know him well enough.

VERGY: And you're interested in him?

RÉMY: He's painting us, sir.

VERGY: Ah, that! Who's speaking to you?

RÉMY: One thing's for sure, it's neither *Madame* nor me!

LA GUIMARD: Tell me, my dear; how long has he abducted your ward for?

VERGY: It's been over a month.

RÉMY: So you're nephew won't be surprised.

VERGY: I only found out about his name and address today by accident!

LA GUIMARD: You've never seen him?

VERGY: Never; and he doesn't know me either; he came in through Valentine's room during the night, and for that, he must have risked his life twenty times over but he was willing to make that sacrifice; I tell you love is an extraordinary character; we used to love that way before the flood.

RÉMY: The flood extinguished all your fire, and so women must be pretty miserable when they see a rainbow in the sky.

LA GUIMARD: And you're going to throw him into jail?

VERGY: I've come to make sure that my ward is still here and…

LA GUIMARD: Give me that signet letter. Once David is in jail, do you think you'll be able to triumph over your ward? On the contrary, her love will only grow stronger, my dear, and you'll never get to the end of it; sooner or later, she'll escape from your house, and the nephew will enjoy a second abduction of his intended before he got the chance to give her a single compliment! Instead of locking up the painter, why don't you use all your powers to send the young girl to a convent? Once there, she'll be under your exclusive control, and little by little her heart might get used to all the slanderous things you'll invent about the painter! Make him out to be unfaithful, oblivious, disloyal; if he's imprisoned, the ward will accuse you of blasphemy, if he's free, she'll eventually believe you, and absence will triumph over love!

RÉMY: Oh woman! Oh devil incarnate! At every moment I fear he's going to grow some cloven hooves!

VERGY: Our beautiful dancer is truly remarkable, and know that your advice will be followed.

RÉMY: Let's get going, and presto, I'm going to make you run for it. Hold your waist in and put a stone in your mouth, and stick out your tongue! That's why dogs are out of breath!

(*They exit speedily.*)

SCENE VII.

LA GUIMARD.

LA GUIMARD: (*Alone.*) All is well! David is all mine! Once Valentine is out of the picture, what do I have to fear? This Vergy came at the right time! – A little later, he would have imprisoned my painter, and my whim would be sitting in the Bastille – well, of course, in that case, I would have demolished the Bastille! I don't know anything about those pure loves that proper young girls are supposed to have, but I promise ours are much better!...and if they don't last a long time, it's because they burn with much more strength! – Once my passing fancy is in the bag labeled forgotten, I'll take up my dancing again much to the joy of poor Sirésol! ... but David won't be sorry he loved me, his love will give him his glory, since he will be listed under an assumed name, I'll definitely force that imbecile Vergy to crown the man I love.

I hear some footsteps. Could it be him? Oh! No! – My heart isn't beating enough!

(*She slowly approaches the back door.*)

SCENE VIII.

GUIMARD, VALENTINE, DAVID.

(*At the same time, the right door opens, Valentine has recognized David's footsteps. She comes out running without noticing la Guimard, and rushes into David's arm as he enters.*)

VALENTINE:	It's him!
DAVID:	My dear Valentine! (*He leads her to the front of the stage.*)
LA GUIMARD:	They haven't seen me at all!
VALENTINE:	Your absence causes me pain and your return brings me such pleasure!
DAVID:	(*He gives her a kiss.*) Dear child. (*He turns around.*) Oh! Excuse me! Madame!
VALENTINE:	Ah! – Well, that's for the best; she saw me in his arms!
DAVID:	I hope you'll forgive me, Madame, for making you wait!

LA GUIMARD: I was on my way, David, my dear!

VALENTINE: If I had known you were here, I would have kept you company!

LA GUIMARD: You wouldn't have been worth going out of your way for.

DAVID: I've been working on your portrait, Madame, it's coming along; I've been putting all my efforts into it, and you'll be happy! My dear sweetie, hand me my palette.

VALENTINE: Here it is, my David. (*To herself.*) I should have just put on some yellow and gray.

DAVID: Madame, I'm at your beck and call! (*La Guimard sits down on the left, David sits in front of his easel; and Valentine near her lover. David paints.*)

VALENTINE: Oh! Madame, you will so enchanted with this painting! – Your portrait is coming along!

LA GUIMARD: Really, my child, it is to your liking!

VALENTINE: I assure you it is! And you won't complain about how long it took to complete.

LA GUIMARD: Time is of no importance in this matter and I worry that haste will harm its effect!

VALENTINE: Haste? But Madame, my David paints even when you aren't here! I'll pose in place of you.

LA GUIMARD: Ah!...

DAVID: For the clothes, Madame, because there is no resemblance in terms of your features and expressions!

LA GUIMARD: (*Turning around.*) Really, my dear!

VALENTINE: Ah! Madame, don't change positions or we'll lose our perspective.

DAVID: That's it, Madame – turn around a little bit!

VALENTINE: As you see, my painter only loves three quarters of you!

LA GUIMARD: (*To herself.*) This silly girl has got to let me take her place!

(*Long silence.*)

VALENTINE: (*Her voice lowered, to David.*) My dearest, would you please hurry up, I beg of you!

DAVID: Why?

VALENTINE: Oh! I'm suffering during this sitting; my whole heart is breaking and I'm about to burst into tears!

DAVID: Child!

VALENTINE: That lady! – I hate her – She looks at you with eyes that frighten me. – Oh I love you, can't you see!

(*She leans against his shoulder. La Guimard gets up abruptly.*)

DAVID: You're tired, Madame!

LA GUIMARD: Yes! I'm tired of resting! And I need movement. (*She goes toward the easel.*) Not bad!...You have talent, my dear, but beware of letting it spill over into this or that passion or the other; your brushes have an independent air to them, and chains must never shackle their future.

VALENTINE: (*Pale.*) Whose slave do you think he is!

LA GUIMARD: Of everything and nothing, my dear; just like an artist; in their heart, they have freedom, but in their heads, slavery! Their feelings are products of chance, and last as long too!

VALENTINE: Chance is another word for providence, and I don't think its existence is limited in any way.

DAVID: That's true, Madame, chance is the *nom de guerre* that God takes when He hides in order to carry out his good deeds!

LA GUIMARD: Fortunately your passions for other people are not anonymous and that, innocent, clumsy as they are, as everything that is new and inexperienced, they act in the light of day! We know that they last, my dear; and what their price is when one's head lowers itself to one's heart.

DAVID: Listen, Valentine, do you think there's any chance that my love might not come to Rome with me?

VALENTINE: To Rome and to the ends of the earth!

LA GUIMARD: To Rome! – The city of pleasures and orgies, of carnivals and debauchery, of masks and delights! Cradle for all enchanting existences, that bore Nero and Lucrezia Borgia.

VALENTINE: No Madame, it is the city of contemplation and work, of religion and prayer, the cradle of a religion made up of charity and hope; that bore St. Peter, and...

DAVID: Valentine, you can add to that city of the arts and memories, that album in which antiquity and the Middle Ages both contributed their most beautiful pages, that immense amalgam of ruins and masterpieces, that had Leo X and Michelangelo.

LA GUIMARD: Hey there, please make my arms a bit rounder, will you! So that people can notice how they're made!

DAVID: I have rarely seen any that could compete with them.

VALENTINE: *(To herself.)* What a nuisance not to have short sleeves!

LA GUIMARD: Oh! My goodness! – But my cleavage isn't showing enough, my dear and tender one; show some more cleavage! Blazes, it looks like I'm afraid to be out in the afternoon sun!

VALENTINE: *(To herself.)* Oh! Those high-collared dresses! Those high-collared dresses!

DAVID: It will be done according to your wishes, Madame.

VALENTINE: *(In a low voice, to David.)* I don't want that! – I don't want that!

GUIMARD: Hunh?

VALENTINE: I said: aren't you worried that it might seem indecent?

LA GUIMARD: Indecent! What's indecency! How can you talk about indecency at the Opera?

VALENTINE: At the Opera!

DAVID: *(In a low voice.)* Get out of here, Valentine!

VALENTINE: No! I'm staying!

LA GUIMARD: (*To herself.*) Ah! You don't want to leave. (*Out loud.*) At the Opera, of course at the Opera; if one takes unimaginable precautions to hide what is hideous, what is beautiful will shine brightly, and three thousand people prostrate themselves before it.

VALENTINE: At the Opera!

LA GUIMARD: But of course, my child, we have our own fashions! Dresses that have no beginning and that are done right away, as Monsieur d'Artois would say![5] – Don't you know that we've lowered the bar on morality, in order to jump over it more easily! I guess you don't know the famous dancer, la Guimard, do you?

VALENTINE: (*Blushing.*) No! No!

DAVID: Valentine!

LA GUIMARD: Ah! My dear, she is beloved, and all the Sophie Arnoulds of the world can't frighten her! Did you know that the Count Artois had been my lover at one point and that there was a failed attempt to abduct him; but I'm not one to let go of my admirers! That's not my style!

VALENTINE: Ah! Madame! What your saying is not dignified.

DAVID: Go home, Valentine, my child! Do you hear me Valentine—go home.

(*Valentine cries as she exits.*)

---

5. Charles, Louis XVI's brother, and the future Charles X. His title then was the Count Artois and although he was only eighteen years old when the play is set, he already had a reputation for womanizing and debauchery. See Berthier in Verne's *Théâtre inédit, op.cit.*, 598.

SCENE IX.

LA GUIMARD, DAVID.

DAVID: Now, Madame, shall we continue with the sitting?

LA GUIMARD: (*Sitting down.*) But you sir, have you rested at least, as fatigue can hit the painter faster than the model!

DAVID: I thank you Madame! – Would you please resume your pose from a few minutes ago!

LA GUIMARD: We other dancers, my dear friend, don't you know that we shouldn't pose! You would have to grab us at the very moment when the entire theatre caves in from all the applause, when the passion that is released from our most enchanting movements embraces a particularly combustible audience.

(*La Guimard allows herself to demonstrate some provocative poses.*)

DAVID: A bit more natural please, in the way your head is tilting and your arms are hanging.

LA GUIMARD: (*She gets up.*) Ah! We're real colleagues aren't we! Dancers and women, we are your living realities! – shouldn't we offer our hand!

(*She extends her hand to him.*)

DAVID: (*Without interrupting what he is painting.*) Oh! I beg of you, don't move, so that I can capture the undulation from your waist.

LA GUIMARD: Come now, my dear, that doesn't make me look good.

DAVID: It does though!

LA GUIMARD: Let's see now! Let me pose my way!

DAVID: No, not at all! I'm telling you; we can see very well that nature isn't the one that made you.

LA GUIMARD: Why?

DAVID: Because, you're the one who makes nature! What are you asking me? Is la Guimard the one who is calling on me, is the dancer the one I have to paint?

LA GUIMARD: I'm calling on you then.

DAVID: I'm asking you that!

LA GUIMARD: I don't resemble myself in these two instances!

DAVID: Not entirely!

LA GUIMARD: Too bad! – Do you prefer the dancer?

DAVID: I don't know her, Madame.

LA GUIMARD: You don't know her!

DAVID: I have to admit, I'm ashamed of it; but that's the case!

LA GUIMARD: Shall I bring her over?

DAVID: That would be pointless Madame, I prefer the model I've had for the last few days.

LA GUIMARD: (*To herself, with rancor.*) Oh I'll get revenge – I'll get revenge. (*She takes a seat and David paints.*) Heart of marble! – Surveyor's eye! Go! What to say? Do you hope to win the next competition?

DAVID: No, Madame.

LA GUIMARD: No! Why not?

DAVID: Because I'll bow down to no one, and I won't go begging to an insolent protector!

LA GUIMARD: You're proud!

DAVID: I'm a man! – I don't grovel! I walk!

LA GUIMARD: Don't you have any completed paintings!

DAVID: I do, Madame! It's here, in the shadows, just like me! It's turning its back on its audience, just like me. I've already entered competitions, and jealousy, hatred, injustice declared me unworthy of them! My painting is here, I look at it from time to time; I'm not sure if it's out of excessive pride, but it seems good and beautiful to me! I'm judging with artistic conscience, and it pleases me; as there are two men in us: the painter, who lives with his palette in his hand, the conscientious judge, the painter's older brother, who approves or disapproves after him; there's some merit in that I think, some research and fame, but everything will remain buried, just like the wonders of Herculaneum beneath the lava of Vesuvius![6] – I have faith, Madame, but a faith that can lift mountains will nevertheless shake this poor dead canvas from its obscure corner as soon as it's born! But let's not talk about that! Sometimes, I'll have a look at my work, and then, the son is no longer embarrassed by the father, and the father isn't embarrassed by the son!

LA GUIMARD: But what if a protector arrived in the shape of a friendship?

---

6. Herculaneum is a Pompeii-like Roman village discovered as preserved ruins from an eruption by Vesuvius and discovered in the eighteenth century.

DAVID: A friendship?

LA GUIMARD: Love!

DAVID: Love! – My love is no less obscure than I am!

LA GUIMARD: Would it displease you then, my dear David, if I took care of your fame?

DAVID: So you would be interested in my fame?

LA GUIMARD: We must be such unworthy creatures that won't just make good running boards.

DAVID: Oh! Madame! – You know that we bow down before you.

LA GUIMARD: Or that people can go by us without looking at us! There is no middle ground! Alas! You can see now why you're not painting the dancer!

DAVID: Please don't bring up such sad subjects, when I have to paint you, Madame; we need to see the playfulness and laughter fluttering about the canvas!

LA GUIMARD: Why, if I want to make a brilliant future for you, that your recognition not despise me one day!

DAVID: You have contempt for me!

LA GUIMARD: Yes, my dear friend, there are in your words an insulting bitterness that doesn't come from the heart, but from the brain, all filled up with worries, and burdened with sadness! – But, thanks to your talent, I forgive your imperfections from a nature easily irritated by so many insurmountable obstacles! Oh! My David, leave it to someone who wants to make the effort, to be famous for having ignited your future, for having championed its merits, and lo… love! Yes, you'll see the good in fallen angels, when all they have are wings, since they can overcome even the most difficult obstacles, bringing along their beloved artist who is good enough to accept their affection and their wings!

(*She leans on David, who has become concerned and pensive.*)

SCENE X.

LA GUIMARD, DAVID, VALENTINE.

VALENTINE: (*She is pale and weak.*) Oh! David! David. (*She staggers.*)

DAVID: (*He picks her up and takes her in his arms.*) Please allow the good angel to pass through, Madame!

(*He takes her into his room.*)

SCENE XI.

LA GUIMARD.

LA GUIMARD: (*Alone.*) He loves her, he still loves her! – He doesn't even look at me, see me, love me! But I love him, I love this painter. I'm losing my mind. To yield to that Valentine! But she was making fun of me! Look how she loves him! I don't love him that much but I'll still have him! After that, the swooning, the fainting, the nervous attacks! He likes that; well then, we'll do some for him, even if it means getting into deep trouble! I must be a horrible person! I don't want this portrait anymore! It's a good thing that they're going to take that Valentine away. Yes! But David won't leave her, he'll hover around that convent all the time! I won't see him anymore. What should I do? What should I do? What should I do?

SCENE XII.

LA GUIMARD, VERGY, SIRÉSOL.

RÉMY: We flew! – Here we are.

LA GUIMARD: That's good! Be quiet.

VERGY: I can't take it anymore – I'm at the end of my rope!

LA GUIMARD: Too bad.

VERGY: Why?

LA GUIMARD: Because it's not all over yet, big guy.

RÉMY: So let's get going.

VERGY: But ….

LA GUIMARD: What have you brought me there?

VERGY: The order to put my ward into a convent.

LA GUIMARD: That's it!

VERGY: That's it!

LA GUIMARD: So what do you want me to do with that?

VERGY: What do you mean, what do I want you to do with it. Do I know?

LA GUIMARD: Do I!

RÉMY: Do we!

VERGY: Ah that! Didn't you tell me it was necessary?

LA GUIMARD: Why, never!

VERGY: For example!

LA GUIMARD: Are you making fun of me!

RÉMY: You're insulting my student.

VERGY: (*To Rémy.*) Will you ever shut up?

RÉMY: Me, shut up!

VERGY: All he does is assault me with jokes all the way through, and he's made me wheezy.

LA GUIMARD: Give me that order! – Shut up Rémy!

VERGY: Here it is!

LA GUIMARD: Do you think that by putting your ward a convent you'll prevent her from corresponding with David! And that he won't abduct her again! Then you don't know how much he loves her – you've forgotten that he's a man with extraordinary audacity to whom no one can give orders! But you must be an idiot, a fool, an imbecile, a madman? Oh what's in that head of yours? What, you carry a signet letter that allows you to imprison David, but you don't do it! – So does that mean you want that man to massacre you, to exterminate you, to kill you! You've had enough of living! Lunatic! Take back this letter. (*She gives him back the signet letter.*) Go run to the police lieutenant, bring him with his men, and in ten minutes, your damned painter will be behind the bars of the Bastille, and we'll see if love can get him out of there.

RÉMY: (*To himself.*) Bravo! Ah, what a woman! She's furious! She hasn't succeeded!

VERGY: But you told me ….

LA GUIMARD: Be quiet!

VERGY: And yet…

RÉMY: Be quiet!

(*Guimard is writing at a table.*)

VERGY: (*In a lower voice to Rémy.*) She does have a point!

RÉMY: Because you always do! Ask Madame de Vergy!

VERGY: Wiseguy!

RÉMY: Calm down! Or I'll beat an *entrechat* into your back!

LA GUIMARD: Go get the police lieutenant; he's devoted to me; he'll get the job done for you and the painter will be in jail before long!

VERGY: Ouf! I can't take it anymore!

LA GUIMARD: Rémy! Go with him!

RÉMY: Done!

VERGY: I'll remember this favor, my cutie!

LA GUIMARD: Good, good! I'll have you crown an anonymous painting.

VERGY: That's a promise.

RÉMY: Let's get going

(*They exit.*)

SCENE XIII.

LA GUIMARD.

LA GUIMARD: (*Alone.*) I've got him! My painter! You're all mine! Vergy will marry off his ward while you're in prison! And be wary of my anger and jealousy so that it won't make your incarceration too long or too hard! We'll see, when you're crowned, if fame and love won't triumph over childhood memories!

SCENE XIV.

LA GUIMARD, DAVID.

DAVID: You'll excuse me, Madame, if I'm unable to finish the sitting, but this poor child is suffering to the point where I can't leave her alone.

LA GUIMARD: My poor friend, you see that I'm in tears!

DAVID: What's the matter with you! What's gotten into you! What are you afraid of?

LA GUIMARD: Nothing for me, but for you.

DAVID: What! Speak up!

LA GUIMARD: You're a goner!

DAVID: A goner!

LA GUIMARD: That Vergy discovered your name and your residence.

DAVID: Valentine's guardian!

LA GUIMARD: He was just here! He got a signet letter against you: you're going to be arrested!

DAVID: Great God! And what about her!

LA GUIMARD: He's taking her with him.

DAVID: Infamy! Oh! My reason! My head! Save her, Madame, my life is in your hands.

LA GUIMARD: What can I do?

DAVID: But she's dying. This will kill her! Valentine! Oh my poor love what will become of you; oh you, the consolation for all my rotten days, the hope of my life, the joy in my sadness, the sun in my darkness, the love of my entire heart, to not see her, to not hear her, to not love her anymore! Infamy! They'll never get her! – They'll never get her!

(*He takes a sword off from the wall.*)

LA GUIMARD: David! A bit of prudence please! Your excesses will tumble down on you! Moderation, patience!

DAVID: You've obviously never loved if you can speak to me with those kinds of words! You've obviously never cried in your entire life, if you can't see what kind of fire burns in my eyes? Ah! Be quiet.

LA GUIMARD: Poor fellow! Poor fellow!

DAVID: Let's get out of here! Let's get out of here!

LA GUIMARD: It's too late!

DAVID: Horrors!

LA GUIMARD: Here they are.

SCENE XV.

LA GUIMARD, DAVID, SIRÉSOL, LIEUTENANT, *soldiers*.

RÉMY: The house is surrounded. All is lost!

LA GUIMARD: Be quiet – be quiet! What about Vergy?

RÉMY: He collapsed from exhaustion on the way over here.

THE LIEUTENANT: Monsieur David, the painter?

DAVID: That's me.

THE LIEUTENANT: Please come with me.

DAVID: Where to?

THE LIEUTENANT: To the Bastille.

DAVID: How come?

THE LIEUTENANT: For having abducted a young girl from her guardian's arms.

DAVID: I'm a goner! Never, sir.

THE LIEUTENANT: You refuse to obey me.

DAVID: I refuse!

THE LIEUTENANT: (*To the others.*) Take this man away!

DAVID: (*His sword is drawn.*) Never!

SCENE XVI.

THE SAME, VALENTINE.

VALENTINE: (*She comes out pale and defeated.*) David! (*She falls into his arms.*)

DAVID: Valentine! They've just arrested me – we'll be separated. She's dying!

VALENTINE: (*Unsteadily.*) Oh! I love you! I love you!

LA GUIMARD: Don't resist David, I'll save her!

DAVID: Farewell! Valentine, farewell! (*He gives her to la Guimard.*) Onwards!

(*They take him away.*)

ACT II

The stage represents la Guimard's splendidly furnished living room. On the left, an easel holding the finished portrait of the famous dancer. Back door.

SCENE I.

LA GUIMARD, SIRÉSOL.

RÉMY: Why what's the matter with you my child? What's happening to you?

LA GUIMARD: Abrecourt and Chandas aren't here!

RÉMY: No! But they'll go mad! You asked to meet with them?

LA GUIMARD: That's good! That's good!

RÉMY: You're getting so skinny! You're leaving! When I keep on repeating to you that you that you didn't dance well last night!

LA GUIMARD: Really?

RÉMY: Really!

LA GUIMARD: Ah! Bah!

RÉMY: What! Do you really want me to die from despair!

LA GUIMARD: You! The only thing that would kill you is a missed entrechat!

RÉMY: Wicked child! You, to whom I inculcated your very first notions of ballet!

LA GUIMARD: Tell me! That Valentine is getting married?

RÉMY: I'm certain she is.

LA GUIMARD: It's been three weeks since she separated from David! She's forgotten him then?

RÉMY: I'm pretty sure! – I won't even give you three days before that painter is erased from your memory.

LA GUIMARD: Are you crazy! Don't you see that I have a fever! That I'm dying!

RÉMY: But he doesn't love you!

LA GUIMARD: He doesn't love me the way I want to be loved!

RÉMY: Didn't you tell him about all the things you did for him?

LA GUIMARD: It's not gratitude that I'm after!

RÉMY: So he has no clue that, along with the police officer you got, you helped him escape to your place!

LA GUIMARD: Do you know that he would have died in the Bastille! He had barely taken refuge here, and he had fallen motionlessly! So many emotions has crushed him! For ten days, his life was hanging by a thread, and my care alone was the only thing that saved him from the jaws of death!

RÉMY: So that's how you became a live-in nurse! You're sinking, my child! You're sinking! Where is that time when with a bow and a scrape you were able

Mademoiselle Guimard as Terpsichore, by Jacques-Louis David.

	to impassion even the most lukewarm of spectators?
LA GUIMARD:	That period has passed! As I no longer love as I once did; I love as I have never loved! – Are you devoted to me, Rémy?
RÉMY:	(*Raising his foot.*) I swear it! And that is a sacred oath.
LA GUIMARD:	Good, I'm counting on you!
RÉMY:	For what?
LA GUIMARD:	You'll find out!
RÉMY:	Very well! My child, some pretty extraordinary things are happening around here! Many secret plans are terrifying me; you're becoming virtuous and you're packing your trunks! Where are you going?
LA GUIMARD:	Nowhere! I'm waiting for my admirers! I brought David's portrait to the competition! David doesn't realize that Valentine's guardian is actually the head of the jury; and he doesn't know that David is the author of the painting. I have his vote; and if Chandas and Abrecourt have kept their word, the entire jury is mine: then we'll see what fame and glory have to offer!
RÉMY:	So you aren't loved, my poor girl! That painter of yours is quite happy, however, in this refuge! – Look at this beautiful portrait he just finished!
LA GUIMARD:	Isn't it pretty? Well then, my poor Rémy, I already don't resemble it! Oh! I'm changing!
RÉMY:	If you only knew how little virtue becomes you!

LA GUIMARD: But I'm not any more virtuous than I was before. I love David!

RÉMY: If you only had three lovers, that would already be more honest; think about it, you only have one.

LA GUIMARD: Did my police lieutenant return the signet letter that he didn't serve?

RÉMY: Here it is.

LA GUIMARD: Good! I also have the order to put the ward into a convent! Everything is in order.

RÉMY: Ah! My dear, you're showing all your cards!

LA GUIMARD: Me! No! I'm going to rip all of this up!

RÉMY: I'll keep all the pieces! Won't you try out this new *pas de deux* that I composed?

LA GUIMARD: Later! Later.

SCENE II.

LA GUIMARD, SIRÉSOL, CHANDAS, ABRECOURT.

LA GUIMARD: Well then?

CHANDAS: Madame!

LA GUIMARD: Hurry up and speak!

ABRECOURT: Victory!

CHANDAS: The members of the jury are all in our court!

ABRECOURT: This representative painting will soon be crowned!

LA GUIMARD: You're sure about that! You'll answer me with your head! Good day.

(*She exits.*)

SCENE III.

SIRÉSOL, CHANDAS, ABRECOURT.

CHANDAS: Well then!

ABRECOURT: Well then?

RÉMY: Ah! Ah! Ah! You've got to be happy.

CHANDAS: Very.

RÉMY: Do you want to meet with her! Well, she is all booked up; very few things in very few words!

ABRECOURT: Everything that la Guimard does is well done!

RÉMY: And so you have helped a lover to escape, to take refuge at his mistresses', to have him crowned, and you're satisfied with all of that!

CHANDAS: Do you take us for idiots?

RÉMY: At best! La Guimard loves David.

CHANDAS: And?

RÉMY:	Now there's one that looks like you. I'll let you guess what Guimard will do with it afterwards! David loves his dancer, as he no longer speaks of his mistress! Either he's been touched by la Guimard's cares or he was shattered by Valentine's wedding, and he needs a major distraction, he loves the dancer!
ABRECOURT:	My dear fellow, we are much cleverer than we appear to be.
RÉMY:	You're right to say so! – Let's see.
CHANDAS:	The jury will crown the painting.
ABRECOURT:	And the painting will be crowned ….
CHANDAS:	David will go to Rome!
RÉMY:	So the travel preparations are for him.
CHANDAS:	No doubt!
ABRECOURT:	And once in Rome, do you think that la Guimard will swear to be faithful to him for five years?

RÉMY:	Her!…This all about her stubbornness which is already beginning to wear her out – and by the way, there's still hope for you! It's love that will supply it! You know the old song:
	
	  "Love makes beasts witty
	  And turns witty people into beasts!"

CHANDAS:	Ah! Ah! Well said! That turns witty people into beasts!
ABRECOURT:	That's us.

RÉMY: That's not what I thought. You are consequently in charge of shipping the little one to Rome! I'll explain the trunks and the mail coach!

ABRECOURT: And it's about time. Did you know that la Guimard was a bit off during last night's performance!

RÉMY: Would you kindly shut up, you fool! – Do you really want lightning to strike you down, your blasphemy and you! – And you allow him to say that.

CHANDAS: Oh, we promised not to fight each other anymore! It's unhealthy and it doesn't amount to much! I've also noticed less lightness and grace from our dancer's pirouettes lately!

RÉMY: Vile ones! Silence! It's true! – But with David gone, she will surely go back to all her glory in executing a new step that I will compose for her!

CHANDAS: Bravo! Dear professor!

RÉMY: The conclusion is admirable; the final group has such an enchanting easy-going-ness about it that it will give my old regulars goose bumps.

ABRECOURT: Is that a fact?

RÉMY: See for yourself! (*He places Abrecourt into Chandras's arms and forces him to bend to such an extent that his feet are higher than his head,*) Oh! Magnificent! Delightful! Divine! I'll go get my dancer.

CHANDAS: Duke!

ABRECOURT: Marquis!

CHANDAS: I would really like to find out if this David loves la Guimard.

ABRECOURT: And whether he no longer loves that Valentine who is about to be married.

SCENE IV.

CHANDAS, ABRECOURT, DAVID.

DAVID: (*Arrives humming a tune.*) Gentlemen, if you would only remain two months in that position, I would turn your embrace into a remarkable painting.

CHANDAS: Until then, my dear painter, your brilliant portrait of our beloved Guimard was a success that is way beyond our expectations.

ABRECOURT: And are you feeling better?

DAVID: Yes, sir.

CHANDAS: That was fast!

DAVID: I felt it went on long enough!

CHANDAS: (*To himself.*) He doesn't love la Guimard.

ABRECOURT: Being away from your studio threw you into a profound sadness.

DAVID: Oh! Not at all, sir!

CHANDAS: Was la Guimard's hospitality a burden to you?

DAVID: On the contrary!

ABRECOURT: Did you consider her a good, generous, devoted woman!

DAVID: My gratitude will know no bounds besides death itself!

ABRECOURT: (*To himself.*) So he does love la Guimard.

CHANDAS: Haven't you forgotten something that was dear to you?

DAVID: Nothing!

CHANDAS: And yet, we knew you when you were quite in love!

DAVID: I was so young at the time! Childhood memories.

ABRECOURT: And yet, this Valentine ….

DAVID: Who! That child? Ours was a unique type of love! It was very tender, but a bit boring.

ABRECOURT: Come now, you haven't forgotten her.

DAVID: No, because to have forgotten her, I would have had to remember her!

CHANDAS: And yet, we admired her face in several of your paintings.

DAVID: Certainly! At that time, I was thinking about it, and when love drives the brush, masterpieces come out of it. But now, I wouldn't be able to reproduce a single feature of hers. (*Pointing to la Guimard's portrait.*) You'd have to be in love to be able to make something worthwhile! That painting is terrible!

CHANDAS:	Oh! There you go, he doesn't love la Guimard then!
DAVID:	I'll start over and now, I'm able to paint a canvas that, were it covered in gold, wouldn't earn a penny.
CHANDAS:	(*To himself.*) He definitely loves her! Oh! I want to be sure… (*Out loud.*) You know, that child!
DAVID:	What child?
CHANDAS:	The one you used to love!
DAVID:	Which one?
CHANDAS:	Why Valentine of course!
DAVID:	What about her?
CHANDRAS:	She's getting married.
DAVID:	That's what they say!
ABRECOURT:	I'm sure of it!
DAVID:	That's a good thing, sir!
CHANDAS:	Today, in fact, if I'm not mistaken.
DAVID:	The competition's today?
CHANDAS:	No! The wedding!
DAVID:	There was a lot of competition!
CHANDAS:	I thought you were the only one!
DAVID:	In that case, I know I'm going to succeed.

ABRECOURT: (*Laughing.*) Are you absolutely sure about that; tonight, there will be an extra one who will be quite happy!

DAVID: Please God that it should be me!

CHANDAS: But you already were, since you loved ….

DAVID: To compete. Indeed, I came in second!

ABRECOURT: Second? – Ah! So you weren't the one who abducted her!

DAVID: First prize? – Alas! – No! I'll be in Rome. – Moreover, if my painting is crowned today, I'll leave tonight, that is to say, we'll both leave!

CHANDAS: Both!

ABRECOURT: Both! Ah! Who are you talking about?

DAVID: And you gentlemen? … Do you want me to kill you, is that what you want!

CHANDAS: We're talking about Valentine.

DAVID: As for me, I'm not talking to you about her!

ABRECOURT: Sir!

DAVID: When I say that I love someone, it's la Guimard I'm talking about, she's the one I can't stop loving, it's la Guimard, whom I will abduct this evening, it's la Guimard!

ABRECOURT: You ought to know that that's not going to happen!

DAVID: It will.

CHANDAS: You should be able to find some sort of sword in some case over there, and some thicket in the garden.

DAVID: I'll find whatever you would like!

ABRECOURT: In a half an hour, sir.

DAVID: Ah, whenever you'd like!

(*They exit.*)

SCENE V.

DAVID.

DAVID: (*Alone, humming through his teeth.*) The fools! I'll wound them! That's all! They're quite happy that I don't love anymore, otherwise I would kill them! Ah! My poor Guimard, how you've changed! – Ah! Well, I don't want her to become too virtuous! – I've had it up to here with virtue! – What I need are orgies, debauchery, that shroud for my heart, because my heart is dead! I'm burying it; and long live God, its funeral will be performed to the tune of full glasses and empty brains! We will have so much fun in Rome! – Mind you, it will be far from Paris! – It seems as though the further we go away, the less we grow nearer! Memory is like rubber; the more we stretch it, the thinner it gets: There's even a moment when it breaks off! – I hope she'll be happy in her marriage! She could have at least made friends with my dancer while I was in the Bastille to console me from afar! – But she didn't come at all! The tart! – If I had her portrait, I'd stomp all over it! I can't remember any of her features. I wouldn't be able to recognize her in the street! One night, a few days ago, when it was dark out, I slipped by Vergy's townhouse! Those wedding noises were all too real! – She might have passed by there, without my having recognized her! – Oh! If I were crowned! Should we ever love anything besides art! As long as nobody arrests me! – Maybe it would be better for me to be buried among the Bastille's jail cells! Oh! I would promptly die! (*He starts crying.*) Die! – But all it would take is to live another way; it's the same thing in the end! – So where is my beautiful dancer? – True God, I would be damned just for her feet! As long as she doesn't ask me for a naïve kind of love again! – My goodness, I don't have any left anymore! I've spent it all! There's something good thrown out the window of unfaithfulness! – Ah! And now's there's a duel to be fought; two duels – Oh! How I would kill them if I were still in love! Ah! My God, as long as they don't pack my sword! My anger would find itself unarmed.

SCENE VI.

DAVID, LA GUIMARD.

LA GUIMARD: What is it, my dear angel?

DAVID: Ah, my sweet! I don't want them to pack my sword away.

LA GUIMARD: Ah, why is that?

DAVID: For goodness' sake, I want to act like a big shot! – Ah, let's leave now!

LA GUIMARD: I think so, I've succeeded.

DAVID: True God!

LA GUIMARD: The jury's votes are in my court.

DAVID: My sweet, I'll pay for that good piece of news in kisses when we are both at the border!

LA GUIMARD: Bah! We'll bust through the border.

DAVID: I'll act like a true smuggler!

LA GUIMARD: Will you be bringing all these canvasses or does every woman's face look alike?

DAVID: Not in the least! That would be too heavy! – We'll make a nice life for ourselves there.

LA GUIMARD: If you'd like, we could have a country house near Rome.

DAVID: A villa with an Italian terrace.

LA GUIMARD: Aren't you going to love Italian faces too much?

DAVID: Come on! Madonnas! – I don't want to hear anything like that again! – When I wanted to paint betrayal, I'll put some blond hair on her, with blue eyes and an oval face. They are ellipses without a home.

LA GUIMARD: So you do love me a little!

DAVID: I wouldn't have it any other way!

LA GUIMARD: I'm not so sure.

DAVID: Nor am I! If I could do it all over again, I would still love you!

LA GUIMARD: Truly?

DAVID: You say that word in such a ravishing manner! Truly! – Well yes, truly, my love!

(*He sighs.*)

LA GUIMARD: What's the matter?

DAVID: Oh! I'm still choking a bit; enormous heat waves in my head! – Oh! Those nerves! I don't know what use they are to men!

LA GUIMARD: To men and to women.

DAVID: Oh! No – the latter need their attacks.

LA GUIMARD: Meanie! – You're provoking me!

DAVID: Will you love but me over there?

LA GUIMARD: What do you mean, love just you?

DAVID: Oh! Don't swear to anything! Don't swear to anything! – It will bring us bad luck.

LA GUIMARD: Well then, why are you asking that?

DAVID: In order not to know the answer!

LA GUIMARD: You deserve an affirmative one.

DAVID: Shush! Promise me just one thing!

LA GUIMARD: What is it?

DAVID: That we don't speak about the future! But your Count Artois will be despondent.

LA GUIMARD: David!

DAVID: He'll drive his sword though his body!

LA GUIMARD: Now it's my turn, promise one thing!

DAVID: What is it?

LA GUIMARD: Let's never talk about the past.

DAVID: You're right, mind you; we have our hands full with the present! Who cares about the rest of it; in the past, we aren't born yet; in the future, we're already dead! What is life? The present.[7] – My dear love, you have thoughts that are filled with philosophy. – What will become of the opera without you?

LA GUIMARD: It will go bankrupt if it wants.

DAVID: But your smiles are the ones that will never run out, and your *ron de jambe* will be the ones that bankrupt them.[8]

---

7. The theme of the present is ubiquitous in Verne's work, most notably in one of his earlier poems called *La Vie* (*Life*) written in 1849 in which he writes:

> The past is not, but it can be painted
> And in a living memory can be seen
> The future is not, but it can be feigned
> Beneath the brilliant traits of a credulous hope!
> Only the present is, but suddenly projects itself
> Like a lightning bolt, at the heart of nothingness!
> Such is existence exactly
> A hope, a point, a recollection.

This is my translation, and the original poem may be found in Jules Verne, *Poésie inédites*, édition dirigée par Christian Robin (Paris: Le Cherche Midi, 1989), 176.

8. *Ron de jambe* is a ballet term for circular leg movements.

LA GUIMARD: No matter, if I pay you exactly what I owe you in love!

DAVID: But, my angel, your abduction will set France on fire; that is to say, the opposite of what you've just said! – I mean, they won't let us leave.

LA GUIMARD: Bah! My mail coach is downstairs with my four best horses!

DAVID: Horses? What are you talking about! You let yourself be pulled by horses? But we'll never get there! – Those animals are very indifferent folks and they don't care if they are pulling a prosecutor or a dancer.

LA GUIMARD: So what do you want me to do!

DAVID: Let me get into your mail coach, unbeknownst to Chandas and Abrecourt. – Get into the seat, harness Abrecourt and Chandras, and you'll see how fast we'll go!

LA GUIMARD: Ah! There! Who is making you so crazy?

DAVID: Me! Crazy!

LA GUIMARD: Yes! Crazy!

DAVID: I have no idea! – Would you know?

LA GUIMARD: (*Sadly.*) My poor friend, I have my doubts!

DAVID: Ah! Great God! Don't forget to bring your most beautiful ballet costumes, I want to paint you in each of your triumphs! – I'll paint your feet, to Sirésol's great pleasure.

LA GUIMARD: (*To herself.*) Alas!

DAVID: By the way! Are you bringing him along!

LA GUIMARD: Yes! He'll ride in the backseat!

DAVID: How many can we fit into the coach?

LA GUIMARD: Just two people, no more than that!

DAVID: Two people!

LA GUIMARD: You wanted us to be three!

DAVID: On the contrary; we should only have had one!

LA GUIMARD: Why is that?

DAVID: Because in places that fit just one person, lovers can hold onto each other very comfortably!

LA GUIMARD: Now there's a bit of wisdom!

DAVID: Oh my God! Madness, wisdom; wisdom, madness, it all goes together! Wisdom is the folly of sages; folly is the wisdom of madmen! Do you really think, my dearest angel, it's so important to acquit or condemn by these types of verdicts life's actions; of course not! – We shouldn't act according to principles; principles lead straight to hell, but rather, we should act by following contexts! – Let's not condemn incomprehensible things, there is often more madness hidden within a wise person, and more wisdom in succumbing to all the instincts of a crazy person! – The most important thing is to be happy, and to be happy, one has to be the man of the hour, looking neither ahead nor behind, one must have equal disdain for both halves of the horizon, but always looking up, towards the zenith; that's where the sun is, and the sun is what youth, enthusiasm and love are made of!

LA GUIMARD: Okay then! I won't ask you if you love me anymore!

DAVID: I would answer no to you, since I love you! – If there's still room in your trunks, stuff a lot of pleasure in them; we'll use it in Rome! – But try to pack as little virtue as possible, it's too hot for those kinds of countries!

LA GUIMARD: In that case, I'll make sure that I put in a good amount of love for you, as you'll die of cold.

DAVID: Come now! – The results will be in at 2 o'clock!

LA GUIMARD: My dear angel! I will be the first to find out!

DAVID: It would give me such pleasure to win first prize!

LA GUIMARD: We'll leave as soon as we find out!

DAVID: Ah, indeed! – Are you the one abducting me or am I the one abducting you?

LA GUIMARD: You're the one who's abducting me, since you're tearing me away from Parisian bravos.

DAVID: You're the one who's abducting me, my cutie, since I'm a resident at the Bastille!

LA GUIMARD: We'll find out if you're leaving the prison voluntarily!

DAVID: And if you willingly abandon the Opera's honors!

LA GUIMARD: There, I believe in something!

DAVID: It's that ….

LA GUIMARD: We're both abducting each other.

DAVID: In that case, we'll fly high!

LA GUIMARD: As long as we leave soon. I'm going to speed everything up! – I would really like to be at the border by now.

DAVID: Why?

LA GUIMARD: You know why, since I'll also be at the border of your indifference! Farewell, my sweet heart!

DAVID: Go on, my cutie!

SCENE VII.

DAVID.

DAVID: (*Alone.*) Oh! How I suffer! – I do hope that fame and triumph will get a chance to swallow me up! I won't leave! – Yes, indeed, I'll leave, as I'll see her again, and if I saw her again I would be finished! – Oh! You really love me, my Guimard; and I'll do everything in my power to love you! – Married! Married, married, and maybe even at this very moment! *Sacre bleu!* And my sword, and my faithful sword!...

SCENE VIII.

DAVID, VERGY.

VERGY:	Excuse me, sir, isn't our beautiful dancer here!
DAVID:	She just left a few minutes ago.
VERGY:	I'll wait for her, sir.
DAVID:	Should she be rushing back here? – Do you have some bad news to report ….
VERGY:	On the contrary, sir, I've come to express my sincere gratitude to her!
DAVID:	Everyone has some for her then! – Whom should I announce is here?
VERGY:	The head of the art jury!
DAVID:	Ah! Monsieur!
VERGY:	Yes! It's me, monsieur!
DAVID:	What we should especially admire in you is the talented painter!
VERGY:	Oh! I wouldn't recognize myself at all, sir.
DAVID:	Really? You surprise me!
VERGY:	Oh! Not at all!
DAVID:	So you judge with absolute impartiality then.
VERGY:	That's true.

DAVID:	You allow yourself to be influenced by neither the correction of the drawing nor the purity of the lines!
VERGY:	In no way at all, sir.
DAVID:	You're not one of those people who swoons before an admirable composition or a vigorous color!
VERGY:	Absolutely not!
DAVID:	You won't look at the most or the least of the harmony of groups?
VERGY:	By no means.
DAVID:	At the more or less happy effects of light!
VERGY:	Obviously!
DAVID:	Finally at the real beauty that makes a painting a first class one!
VERGY:	Sir, you have happily painted the portrait of the noble independent thinking that makes me such a conscientious judge!
DAVID:	Please do have a seat, sir! (*They sit down.*) And were the paintings that were submitted all remarkable?
VERGY:	Yes and no! – I hardly got a chance to look at them, and yet, I still prefer new paintings to old stuffy ones from what we call the masters! I infinitely prefer those wonderfully rosy and vivacious faces!
DAVID:	What you're saying to me now doesn't surprise me in the least. – And have you picked the winner yet?

VERGY: No doubt; and I've just spoken about it with la Guimard; she recommended a painting to me, and her recommendation holds sway.

DAVID: I'm interested, sir.

VERGY: By an unusual set of circumstances, the judgment of my colleagues coalesced around the same painting; these are old examiners in whom one can have absolute confidence!

DAVID: Have you been newly minted in this important position?

VERGY: This very year, sir; this very year!

DAVID: And what's the name of the happy painter?

VERGY: I don't know it! It's an anonymous painting ….

DAVID: Sir, I'm refraining from going for your neck, only because I'm afraid of choking you!

VERGY: Sir.

DAVID: Sir, I am la Guimard's *protégé*, the author of the painting you speak of!

VERGY: And which will be crowned the winner, I am sure of it, when my voice supports it in a few minutes!

DAVID: Sir, you are a man who is worthy of public esteem.

VERGY: That's the good news that I wanted to share with la Guimard.

DAVID: This generous woman has done me a great favor then.

VERGY:	Indeed, sir; as a result of unique circumstances where chance allowed me to meet her.
DAVID:	Sir, I'm not asking for any details!
VERGY:	But it's really strange; she hadn't actually suggested, but practically helped me put a certain individual behind bars at the Bastille.
DAVID:	The Bastille!
VERGY:	And in fact, it was a painter just like you! A tramp, a man with no talent at all, who had the audacity to abduct my niece!
DAVID:	Monsieur de Vergy!
VERGY:	That's my name! – There's nothing strange in your knowing it; if he had entered a competition, he would have been rejected.
DAVID:	He would have been one less adversary.
VERGY:	A rather unimpressive adversary; I put him in jail, and I'm marrying my ward off to my nephew!
DAVID:	So she's getting married.
VERGY:	Today!
DAVID:	She's gotten over me.
VERGY:	Very promptly sir, sir; very promptly – I was very strict with her at first, but now she is free and is getting married this evening.
DAVID:	Oh! I'm dying! I'm dying! – And so the poor devil is in prison!

VERGY: Yes! We'll leave him there for a few years, he's a rotten apple!

DAVID: Monsieur de Vergy, I am David, the painter, and you are a scoundrel!

VERGY: You!

DAVID: And I should shoot you down on the spot like a dog!

VERGY: You frighten me, sir!

DAVID: Tremble with fear then; as you have reason to tremble.

(*He puts his hand on his shoulder.*)

VERGY: Help, somebody help me! Murderer!

DAVID: Wretch! You won't escape me.

SCENE IX.

DAVID, VERGY, LA GUIMARD.

LA GUIMARD: Ah! Good God! – All is lost!

VERGY: It's a betrayal, Madame!

LA GUIMARD: David! David.

DAVID: Fear not, my cutie! – I won't touch him any longer! – Go ahead and marry off your ward, do you hear me! – I hate her! – I more than hate her in fact; I have contempt for her!

VERGY: But!

DAVID: Not a word! – And as for you, my poor beloved, you would have lost your generous pain! I would have sacrificed my fame to my wrath; but we'll flee together, as I love you and will always love you!

LA GUIMARD: Oh! My David, thank you! – Do you hear that! He loves me!

DAVID: I love her! See you soon.

(*He exits after having kissed her.*)

SCENE X.

VERGY, LA GUIMARD.

VERGY: But it's a horror, an indignity.

LA GUIMARD: Calm down, my fat friend!

VERGY: But I've been tricked in a very undignified manner!

LA GUIMARD: Like an old instrument!

VERGY: That is to say you led me to a police officer from one of your friends to escort this goofball to your place!

LA GUIMARD: Be careful, what if he heard you!

VERGY: That's true! But I'll still have him hanged!

LA GUIMARD: Stay!

VERGY: And I'll speak to other criminal lieutenants since you know everyone.

LA GUIMARD: Exclude yourself!

VERGY: What do you mean!

LA GUIMARD: Yes! I thought I knew you better. But you don't understand a thing!

VERGY: I understand just one thing—That he's going to take off now that he knows he's been found out!

LA GUIMARD: But he truly believes that he's escaped very adroitly from the hands of soldiers; he imagines he's still struck with a signet letter.

VERGY: But he most certainly is!

LA GUIMARD: Not really! Since I have it on me!

VERGY: But that's odious, Madame!

LA GUIMARD: Sir, can't you see that I love him, and you can guess that he'll flee me.

VERGY: You think you can convince me that he's more in chains near you than in the Bastille!

LA GUIMARD: Such a beautiful thing the Bastille! – It isn't a place no one gets out of – But love is another matter!

VERGY: So he loves you!

LA GUIMARD: You heard him!

VERGY: That gets me angry; but he just insulted me in a completely revolting manner! Why wouldn't I get revenge?

LA GUIMARD: You won't get revenge!

VERGY: First of all, my niece is getting married today.

LA GUIMARD: That's exactly what's needed!

VERGY: My goodness, I'm the one who came up with such lies against this David, that convinced Valentine that he was cheating on her while they were together, I was hardly wrong in doing so.

LA GUIMARD: Enough about that! – David is a free man, he loves me; and it is in your interest that everything turned out this way.

VERGY: You'll never be able to prove that to me!

LA GUIMARD: Do you think he wouldn't have left your prison one day or another; what would you have said if, after several years in captivity, breathing anger, hatred, vengeance, he would have found himself betrayed himself, deceived, tormented, face to face with you, his traitor, his deceiver and his torturer?

VERGY: You're scaring me! – When you put it that way, it's rather awkward.

LA GUIMARD: He's happy then that everything turned out this way, and as for your ward, she will hate him because he loves me, and you too because you no longer fear her hateful appearances!

VERGY: By Jove, you're right, and for all my vengeance's sake, I'll take his painting out of the competition.

LA GUIMARD: You wouldn't do that!

VERGY: What do you mean, I wouldn't do that!

LA GUIMARD: No!

VERGY: You, the strong one.

LA GUIMARD: Quite sensible, no doubt.

VERGY: What, you think I'll crown him!

LA GUIMARD: You'll crown him.

VERGY: Me, Vergy, whom you called a wretch, to whom he was terribly rude, etc., you think I would give him the grand prize!

LA GUIMARD: Of course!

VERGY: Here, I'm leaving, as you'll be capable of convincing me that I should still have an interest in him!

LA GUIMARD: Obviously!

VERGY: Ah, the more he mistreats me, the more I have to do him favors, and all that is in my interest.

LA GUIMARD: Listen! Once he gets the Institute Prize, where's he going?

VERGY: To Rome!

LA GUIMARD: How many miles is Rome from Paris?

VERGY: I don't know; but it's very far.

LA GUIMARD: Well then, I'm following him to Rome because I love him! Be quiet! I love him! Do you think that seeing your ward could awaken feelings of revenge in him; do you think your meeting him could suddenly put ideas of rather legitimate hatred into his brain? Do you think that by keeping him in Paris you're not exposing yourself to one day running into him and having him cut you up into pieces? – Could you ever feel at ease knowing that in any given square he might pop up, dreaming of dark matters, in each street, you might see him pursuing you with deathly looks, at each intersection, you would see him raising a vengeful hand against you! – You're sacrificing your own tranquility then! And with one word, you could avoid all these worries, and put an end to an eternal hatred for ever, and all by pushing him away from you, you could actually be connected to him with ties of gratitude instead – But the more you dawdle, the more you compromise your peace of mind! Who know if he'd accept your protection anymore; you are unbelievably imprudent; but before you have time to see him again, he should be already far away, named, crowned, acclaimed, beatified; and I hereby declare that if in fifteen minutes you haven't brought me his crown, I'll kill myself in despair, and since he'll no longer have anything left to love on this earth, he'll allow his heart to overflow with feelings of hatred, jealousy, vengeance and ferociousness. And then woe onto you!

VERGY: Mercy! Mercy! I'm going, I'm running, I'm judging, I'm crowning, I'm coming back!

LA GUIMARD: Go then! So go off then!

(*She pushes him.*)

SCENE XI.

LA GUIMARD.

LA GUIMARD: (*Alone.*) Finally! – He'll owe his fame to me, just as I owe my happiness to him! – He loves me! He loves me! – Oh! I feel a new life warming my sleepy blood! – He's opened up that grave of indifference I had jumped in from head to toe! – I feel that my heart is reborn today! I see it blossom from love's breath! Oh! Thank you my David! – I love him, I love him! – That young girl must have only had affection for him; she thinks that her lover is guilty, without any proof of it! – Even if I saw it myself, I still wouldn't believe it because I only have one prayer, one religion, one hope, faith in love! – I understand all its intoxication, its passion, its momentum and happiness laden in its quivers from a soul who has been entrenched in herself up until now, in the secret agitation of a dead heart amidst only semblances of love! – He's mine, he loves me! I'm his, his alone; I love him!

SCENE XII.

LA GUIMARD, VALENTINE.

LA GUIMARD: Valentine!

VALENTINE: Ah! Madame! – I see you!

LA GUIMARD: You! You! Oh! What a blow! Oh!

VALENTINE: What's gotten into you?

LA GUIMARD: Nothing! I – nothing; sit down! What do you want here? What do you want from me?

VALENTINE: I've come to cry before you, Madame, and to speak with you about the poor prisoner. If you only knew how I'm dying! And how much strength of will, energy, and heart to suppress the tears that were overflowing from my eyes! I would have run towards you so many times if I hadn't been imprisoned in a damned house, if I hadn't been locked up by order of the very person who would have killed me in this world! Did you know that I devoured my sighs, little by little; I transformed myself into a laughing, amiable, happy girl, that I saw a young man that I hated, that Vergy's nephew, the one who courted me so assiduously, stamp out my protests, burn me with declarations? Did you know that in order to obtain a bit of freedom, I said that I understood, accepted everything…

LA GUIMARD: So are you married?

VALENTINE: …and that I have to get married this very night! Oh! Madame! My weaknesses have been exploited! – against my David, they piled on lie after lie, in front of me, he was accused of treason; they showed me proofs of his infidelity, and I didn't believe any of it because I love him!

LA GUIMARD: She loves him! – I'm going to faint!

VALENTINE: Finally, at the first whiff of freedom, I ran to you! To speak to you about this, to swear that I would rather die than belong to another, to swear to you that I love him!

LA GUIMARD: Alas! What do you want me to tell you? – What do you want me to do for David?

VALENTINE: That you speak to me about his situation! Where is he? – What became of him? – Have you seen him? Can I reach him! – Oh! Madame, you are so powerful, open the doors of the prison for me, so that I can stay there for the rest of my days! Have pity, pity!

LA GUIMARD: What do you want me to say to you, Madame, you keep hitting your head against impossibilities!

VALENTINE: Oh! My God! – I came back to my studio, the place we were so happy in, where we thought we would live happily until the end of time! Once there, I found empty rooms, our little room was empty, my poor flowers faded, and my little birds dead! And it seemed to me as though David was dead as well! He's not dead is he?

LA GUIMARD: No! No!...

VALENTINE: So I got this idea; to make him as happy as possible for the duration of his captivity. You'll help me, Madame, won't you?

LA GUIMARD: Speak up! What is this?

VALENTINE: He's not in love with you at least? – Because in every woman, I think I see a rival ever since I wasn't near him!

LA GUIMARD: No! He doesn't love me!

VALENTINE: And he couldn't love you, as your loves are too unimportant! – Forgive me, I'm speaking to the dancer, I ask forgiveness from the woman!

LA GUIMARD: Come now! What is it that you want in the end?

VALENTINE: Monsieur de Vergy is head to the jury of the competition this year; if we can have his painting crowned, we will give him back some of his happiness!

LA GUIMARD: But…

VALENTINE: Wouldn't he be happy if the wind that blows through his metal bars brought him a bit of fame along with its icy breath?

LA GUIMARD: It's just that…I don't know! ….

VALENTINE: Madame!

LA GUIMARD: Well then! It's already done!

VALENTINE: He's been crowned?

LA GUIMARD: Yes!

VALENTINE: Without me! (*Silence.*) Without me. By you! (*Silence.*) Why! (*Silence.*) You love him then! Answer me, so you love him! (*Valentine turns around, and finds herself facing la Guimard's portrait.*) Ah! He's here! – He's here! That portrait! That completed portrait!

LA GUIMARD: But Madame!

VALENTINE: He's here, I tell you.

LA GUIMARD: I assure you! ….

VALENTINE: (*Calling out.*) David! David!

LA GUIMARD: Silence, Madame!

VALENTINE: Silence yourself, he should hear me! David!

LA GUIMARD: Will you be quiet!

VALENTINE: David! David!

LA GUIMARD: Mine!

SCENE XIII.

LA GUIMARD, VALENTINE, SIRÉSOL.

VALENTINE: Where's David?

RÉMY: Her!

LA GUIMARD: Gag her for goodness' sakes!

VALENTINE: David!

RÉMY: He's not coming back. When Chandas and Abrecourt found out that you were going off with him!...

VALENTINE: With him!

RÉMY: They provoked him; and they're dueling in the garden!

VALENTINE: Ah!

(*She bolts.*)

LA GUIMARD: Oh! She'll get there before I will!

(*La Guimard exits listlessly.*)

SCENE XIV.

SIRÉSOL.

SIRÉSOL: What's going to happen? – It's all for the best! Guimard can't leave! – She won't leave! What's going to happen? Where did that young girl come from? – What if la Guimard killed herself? Oh! – La Guimard who is light as a feather should be the first to arrive.

SCENE XV.

SIRÉSOL, DAVID, VALENTINE.

(*David hold Valentine in his arms.*)

DAVID: Wounded! Wounded!

SIRÉSOL: Wounded!

DAVID: She threw herself between us and yelled: "I love you, David, I'm yours!" – Valentine! Valentine! Come back to life! – Get some help! – Valentine!

SCENE XVI.

SIRÉSOL, DAVI, VALENTINE, LA GUIMARD, ABRECOURT, CHANDAS.

(*La Guimard enters barely keeping herself up; when she sees David and Valentine, she straightens up like a hyena. Chandas's arm is in a sleeve, and Abrecourt is limping.*)

LA GUIMARD: Woe! Woe to them!

DAVID: Valentine! My poor child. – I'm going to die too if you don't come back to life, if you don't ever see me again, if you no longer tell me "I love you"!

VALENTINE: Am I dreaming? – David!

(*She throws herself around his neck.*)

DAVID: Oh! My beloved!

RÉMY: What's la Guimard going to do?

CHANDAS: The lovers are goners!

SCENE XVII.

THE SAME, VERGY.

VERGY: Victory! Victory! – David has been crowned!

DAVID: Crowned?

VALENTINE: Ah! God is just!

VERGY: Valentine!

VALENTINE: Monsieur de Vergy! We're goners!

DAVID: Fear not, Valentine.

VERGY: (*To la Guimard.*) Is this yet another betrayal? – After locking him up at your place in cahoots with the police lieutenant ….

DAVID: (*To la Guimard.*) You did that!

VERGY: And all of that with the pretext of taking him away from my ward as she was getting married!

DAVID: You did all that! Oh! I despise you!

LA GUIMARD: Enough with the insults! Do you really think one can play with a woman's love with impunity, because I love you, David.

VALENTINE: Silence, Madame! You do not love him!

LA GUIMARD: Oh! He doesn't love me. He'll never love me!

RÉMY: They're goners!

VERGY: Finally! We're all together! Woe to you!

LA GUIMARD: Here is the order to place this woman into a convent! Here's the signet letter against David the painter! Defy me, if you dare to now!

VALENTINE: Oh! Pity! Have pity, Madame, or I'll die!

DAVID: Get back up, Valentine!

LA GUIMARD: Oh!

VALENTINE: I'm giving way.

LA GUIMARD: (*She hands the two letters to Vergy.*) Here! – Now act!

VERGY: Finally! We've got our revenge!

(*Vergy exits.*)

SCENE XVIII.

THE SAME, *minus* VERGY

DAVID: She's dying: are you happy!

LA GUIMARD: Ah! – There's a mail carriage downstairs, leave with her; you're a free man; go to Rome, filled with the happiness of fame and love. There's still Guimard the dancer!

VALENTINE: (*She falls to her feet.*) Oh! Thank you Madame!

LA GUIMARD: I'm the one who told her to get up now!

DAVID: Be blessed, Madame, and may our thanksgiving bring you happiness.

LA GUIMARD: Me and many others! – Isn't that right old bean?

RÉMY: Yes, yes! –I'm crying – My legs are giving way.

LA GUIMARD: Why don't you come over here and show me your *pas de deux*! Your arm, Abrecourt. – Nicely wrapped up in a sleeve; good! – Yours, Chandas. Ah! Now there, I no longer have any lovers! Ah yes, over there! (*To the audience.*) Here are my true lovers, you gentlemen, show me then, by coming here every day, that you are not lame, and, by applauding me, you are not armless.

THE END

Illustrations

ONE OF THE CHALLENGES in the Palik series is selecting illustrations. They are either derived from the first French publication of Verne stories and plays in the 19th century, or are selected from sources of the time depicting actual historical locales, persons or events. *An Excursion at Sea*, in particular, allowed inclusion of engravings from Verne novels and plays, including early British editions never reproduced before, along with illustrations to accompany the various factual allusions in the text. This approach also highlights the echoes of *An Excursion at Sea* in later Verne writing.

For illustrations from the original publications of Verne, the North American Jules Verne Society is indebted to Bernhard Krauth, chairman of the German Jules-Verne-Club. Intensely interested in the illustrations of the original French editions of Verne's work, he has been deeply involved in a project to digitize the illustrations, more than 5,000 in all.

Additional illustrations were provided by Verne bibliographer, Stephen Michaluk, Jr., and renowned Verne biographer Volker Dehs, to whom the North American Jules Verne Society is indebted for advice and assistance in the Palik series.

The cover is a design from a Hetzel French edition, and the scan was provided by Brian Kutzera especially for this Palik series volume.

Acknowledgements

THE PALIK SERIES, while spearheaded by the North American Jules Verne Society, represents a cooperative effort among Vernians worldwide, pooling the resources and knowledge of the various organizations in different countries. The Society is grateful for research assistance to Frédéric Jaccaud, curator of Jean-Michel Margot's Verne Collection at the Maison d'Ailleurs (House of Elsewhere) in Yverdon-les-Bains, Switzerland.

The City of Nantes (France) and its Municipal Library have placed all Jules Verne manuscripts online. They helped make this publication possible, and the Society would like to thank the City of Nantes and its Bibliothèque municipale (Agnès Marcetteau, director) for their ongoing assistance with the Palik Series.

The Society also appreciates the efforts of members who have contributed to this volume, including Jean-Pierre Picot, Terry Harpold, Tad Davis, Jan Rychlík and Jean-Michel Margot, and proofreading assistance was provided by Alex Kirstukas. The translator would like to also thank all of the North American Jules Verne Society members present at the 2016 meeting in Philadelphia, when this volume in the Palik Series was first outlined and presented.

Contributors

PETER SCHULMAN earned his doctorate in French and Romance Philology from Columbia University, and is Professor of French and International Studies at Old Dominion University. He is Chevalier de l'Ordre des Palmes Académiques and the author of *The Sunday of Fiction: The Modern French Eccentric* (Purdue University Press, 2003) as well as *Le Dernier Livre du Siècle* (Romillat, 2001) with Mischa Zabotin. He has edited a critical edition of Jules Verne's *The Begum's Millions* (Wesleyan University Press, 2005) and recently translated Jules Verne's novel *The Secret of Wilhelm Storitz* (University of Nebraska Press, 2012) as well as a meditation on waves by Marie Darrieussecq, *On Waves* (VVV editions, 2014); *Suburban Beauty* from poet Jacques Reda (VVV editions, 2009) and *Adamah* from poet Celine Zins (Gival Press, 2010) and Ying Chen's collection of haiku *Impressions of Summer* (Finishing Line Press, 2016). He is currently co-editor in chief of a new journal of eco-criticism, *Green Humanities* with Josh Weinstein (Virginia Wesleyan College) and has co-edited the following books: *The Marketing of Eros: Performance, Sexuality and Consumer Culture* (Die Blaue Eule, 2003); *Chasing Esther: Jewish Expressions of Cultural Difference* (Kol Katan Press, 2007) and *Rhine Crossings: France and German in Love and War* (SUNY Press, 2004). His translation of Marie Nimier's play *Another Year, Another Christmas* (*Noel revient tous les ans*) was recently performed by the Haberdasher Theater company in Columbus Ohio and New York City in November 2017.

Brian Taves (Ph.D., University of Southern California) was an archivist in the Motion Picture, Broadcasting, and Recorded Sound Division of the Library of Congress for over a quarter century. He is the author of more than 100 articles and 25 chapters in anthologies, and has written books on P.G. Wodehouse and Hollywood; director Robert Florey; the genre of historical adventure movies; and fantasy-adventure writer Talbot Mundy, in addition to editing an original anthology of Mundy's best stories. In 2002-2003, Taves was chosen as Kluge Staff Fellow at the Library to write the first book on silent film pioneer Thomas Ince, published in 2011. In 2015, Taves's *Hollywood Presents Jules Verne: The Father of Science Fiction on Screen* was published by University Press of Kentucky. Taves was coauthor of *The Jules Verne Encyclopedia* (Scarecrow, 1996), and editor of the first English-language publication of Verne's *Adventures of the Rat Family* (Oxford, 1993), before becoming editor of the Palik series.

The Palik Series

THE LAST TWO DECADES have brought astonishing progress in the study of Jules Verne, with new translations of Verne stories, including the discovery of many texts. Still, there remain a number of Verne stories that have been overlooked, and it is this gap that the North American Jules Verne Society seeks to fill in the Palik series.

The North American Jules Verne Society (NAJVS) was formed in 1993, and a decade later, underwrote *Journey Through the Impossible*, the first complete edition in any language of Verne's 1882 science fiction theatrical spectacle, *Voyage à travers l'impossible*. With this experience, and thanks to the generosity of the Society's late member, Edward Palik, a series was commenced to bring to the Anglophone public a series of hitherto unknown Verne tales, published by BearManor Fiction.

Edward D. Palik (1928-2009) was a physicist who had a special enthusiasm for bringing neglected Verne stories to English-speaking readers, and this will be reflected in the series that bears his name. In this way the Society hopes to fulfill the goal that Ed's consideration has made possible, along with the assistance of a variety of Verne translators and scholars from around the world. The volumes in the Palik series will reveal the amazing range of Verne's storytelling, in genres that may surprise those who only know his most famous stories. We hope to allow a better appreciation of the famous writer who has, for more than a century and a half, been the widest-read author of fiction in the world.

Editor of the Palik series is Brian Taves.

Previous Volumes in the Palik Series

The Marriage of a Marquis

Foreword by Brian Taves; Introduction by Walter James Miller; *The Marriage of Mr. Anselme des Tilleuls* translated by Edward Baxter, with a preface and notes by Jean-Michel Margot; Afterword by Edward Baxter; Appendix: *Jédédias Jamet, or The Tale of an Inheritance* translated, with a preface and annotations, by Kieran M. O'Driscoll.

Jules Verne is the acclaimed author of such pioneering science fiction as *Twenty Thousand Leagues under the Seas* and *Journey to the Center of the Earth*. Yet he also wrote much more, and foreshadowing such classics as *Around the World in Eighty Days*, this inaugural volume focuses on two of Verne's earliest humorous stories, *The Marriage of Mr. Anselme des Tilleuls* and *Jédédias Jamet, or The Tale of an Inheritance*. Mr. Anselme des Tilleuls, in the featured story, is a ridiculous young man seeking a bride, following the advice of his Latin tutor to utilize the maxims of that language in his courtship. Translation is provided by Edward Baxter and Kieran O'Driscoll, two of the leading Verne experts; critical commentary by Jean-Michel Margot, Walter James Miller, and Brian Taves examine both stories, and why some of the author's tales were overlooked for so many years.

Shipwrecked Family: Marooned with Uncle Robinson

Translated by Sidney Kravitz; Introduction by Brian Taves.

Castaway by pirates on a deserted island … without tools or supplies to survive … a mother and her children have only a kindly old sailor to help. But what explains the strange flora and fauna they find?

The second volume in the Palik series was rejected by Verne's publisher, so rather than finish it, he began to rewrite it with new characters—and that became the classic, *The Mysterious Island*, where Captain Nemo made his last appearance. Here, then, is Verne's first draft of that novel, one which is very different from the book that it became.

Translation is provided by Sidney Kravitz, also translator of the definitive modern edition of *The Mysterious Island* (Wesleyan University Press, 2002). The introduction by Brian Taves discusses the influence of the Robinsonade on Verne's oeuvre, while an appendix comprises Verne's own prefaces to two of his novels in the genre, describing the influence of the form on his writing.

Mr. Chimp & Other Plays

By Jules Verne with Michel Carré, Charles Wallut, and Victorien Sardou; Translated by Frank Morlock; Introduction by Jean-Michel Margot.

Long before Verne stories had formed the basis for such movies as *Around the World in 80 Days*, many of his plays were theatrical blockbusters on the 19th century stage, including several from his novels. Even as he became a novelist, the stage remained crucial to Verne. In this volume, expert scholarly research by Jean-Michel Margot introduces four of Verne's plays written early in his career, from 1853 to 1860. The four plays are translated by Frank Morlock, one of the most prolific modern translators of 19th century French drama. Included in this volume are: *The Knights of the Daffodil* and *Mr. Chimpanzee*, co-authored by Verne with Michel Carré; *An Adoptive Son*, co-authored by Verne with Charles Wallut, and *Eleven Days of Siege*, co-authored by Verne with Charles Wallut and Victorien Sardou. The works range in content from romantic comedies to a scientist's discovery that there may not be much difference between human and ape after all!

The Count of Chanteleine: A Tale of the French Revolution

Translated by Edward Baxter; Introduction by Brian Taves; Notes and maps by Garmt de Vries-Uiterweerd; Afterword by Volker Dehs.

This adventure, first published in France in 1864 but never before available in English, is for everyone who has thrilled to *The Scarlet Pimpernel*, *A Tale of Two Cities*, or *Scaramouche*. A nobleman, the Count of Chanteleine, leads a rebellion against the revolutionary French government. While he fights for the monarchy and the church, his home is destroyed and his wife murdered by the mob. Now he must save his daughter from the guillotine. This exciting swashbuckler is also a meticulous historical re-creation of a particularly bloody episode in the Reign of Terror.

Commentary by an international team of experts including Garmt de Vries-Uiterweerd, Volker Dehs and Brian Taves explores the historical background, composition, and generic context of *The Count of Chanteleine*, translated by Edward Baxter.

The Count of Chanteleine is also available in a full-length professional reading by the noted vocal artist, Fred Frees, on audible.com.

Vice, Redemption and the Distant Colony

By Jules Verne with Michel Verne; *Pierre-Jean, The Somber Fate of Jean Morénas*, and *Fact-Finding Mission* translated, with an introduction and annotations, by Kieran M. O'Driscoll.

Literary fraud or filial devotion? This is the question at the heart of a firestorm that erupted when manuscripts and letters were discovered proving that Jules Verne's son, Michel, significantly revised over a dozen of the stories published posthumously under his father's name, and even originated some himself. It was a collaboration that had begun while both were still alive, and continued as Michel was his father's literary executor.

In this volume will be found two different versions of a story, as written by Jules (*Pierre-Jean*), and expanded by his son (into *The Somber Fate of Jean Morénas*)—a tale Michel even made as a full-length movie in 1916. Also in these pages is the first English translation of a novel Jules began, *Fact-Finding Mission*, but which his son finished, and hitherto has been only available in the completed version by Michel Verne.

The English rendering and notes are by a leading Verne translator and expert on the history of Verne translations, Kieran O'Driscoll.

Around the World in 80 Days—The 1874 Play

By Jules Verne and Adolphe d'Ennery; The original translation commissioned by the Kiralfy Brothers; Introduction by Philippe Burgaud, with Jean-Michel Margot and Brian Taves; Afterword: "The Meridians and the Calendar" by Jules Verne, translated and annotated by Jean-Louis Trudel; Appendix: The Play on Screen, by Brian Taves.

Jules Verne's most famous novel was originally conceived as a play—and immediately after writing the novel, Verne himself adapted his story into a stage hit. Running for thousands of performances in many different countries, including the United States, here is the original playscript, translated directly from the French by the producers of the original Broadway presentation, and only issued in the most limited form in 1874. Like filmmakers after him, Verne understood the need to make changes for the stage, and in collaboration with Adolphe d'Ennery created a distinct variation, a play with many different characters and episodes than are in the novel, *Around the World in Eighty Days*. Included in this volume are an introduction about how the play was created and staged, together with the first translation (by Jean-Louis Trudel) of Verne's 1873 essay, "The Meridians and the Calendar," explaining how Phileas Fogg accomplished his feat. Background on the production of the play, especially its staging in the United States, is provided by Philippe Burgaud, Jean-Michel Margot, and Brian Taves, along with an appendix on films of the play.

Bandits & Rebels

"San Carlos" and *The Siege of Rome* translated by Edward Baxter; With "Future of the Submarine;" Introduction by Daniel Compère, translated by Jean-Michel Margot with Brian Taves; Appendix: *Martin Paz, or The Pearl of Lima*, the 1852 translation by Anne T. Wilbur of the original French magazine edition.

Captain Nemo's *Nautilus* in *Twenty Thousand Leagues under the Seas* was not the first undersea craft imagined by Jules Verne! A decade earlier, the prophetic author wrote *San Carlos*, imagining a Spanish smuggler who utilizes a vehicle capable of diving beneath the surface of the waves. This newly-discovered story is published here in English for the first time—together with Verne's final words before his death on the future of the submarine as an instrument of war. Also in this volume is another never-before-translated tale, *The Siege of Rome*, a historical adventure of love and betrayal as Garibaldi's revolutionaries are defeated in 1849. Sorbonne professor Daniel Compère introduces the expert translations by Edward Baxter.

Since *Bandits & Rebels* emphasizes two Verne stories written early in his career, but remained unpublished during his lifetime, this volume also includes *Martin Paz*, another story of the same genre but which did appear in the 1850s, in both France and the United States. Reprinted here for the first time from the original translation, this preserves in unvarnished form Verne's own first version of *Martin Paz* to American readers. Previously, only the more polished version rewritten in the 1870s has appeared in book form.

Golden Danube

Translated, with an introduction and annotations, by Kieran M. O'Driscoll.

Jules Verne's "Extraordinary Journeys" often used the travelogue mode, and here the author offers a voyage down the entire length of the Danube, from Germany to the Black Sea. However, rather than the placid "blue" Danube of classical conception, the author offers one which is golden, in multiple ways. Smugglers are operating along the river, with the police in pursuit, and the hero is a champion fisherman who is abducted and forced to prove his courage.

The English rendering and notes are by a leading Verne translator and expert on the history of Verne translations, Kieran O'Driscoll.

A Priest in 1835

Translated with an introduction and notes by Danièle Chatelain and George Slusser.

Here is not only a treasure, but a literary revelation—the very first novel by Jules Verne. Finished by the age of 20 and under the influence of Edgar Allan Poe, *A Priest in 1835* was composed before Verne encountered any editors to hone his storytelling skills. Yet this tyro effort is a masterpiece, a novel told in a modernist style with a nonlinear narrative. This first English translation, with extensive critical commentary, redeems *A Priest in 1835* from the neglect and misunderstanding of French critics, who mistook its contemporary approach for an unfinished work. Instead, Verne reveals that he had not only the prophetic skills that would render him the father of science fiction, but a technique that would win him a place among the vanguard of 21st century authors.

Danièle Chatelain (University of Redlands) and the late George Slusser (University of California, Riverside) are renowned translators and scholars of the early history of science fiction.

Castles of California

Two plays by Jules Verne, *The Castles of California* and *A Nephew from America*, translated with an introduction and notes by Kieran M. O'Driscoll; Appendix: "Jules Verne's Trip to America" by Brian Taves.

Two of Jules Verne's plays have long piqued the interest of American readers, and are included in this volume in translation for the first time. Both feature Frenchmen, recently returned from the United States, discovering the ephemeral nature of wealth. In *The Castles of California*, the Frenchman has come from the California gold fields—has he struck it rich, or has he had the bad luck that befell most of the "Forty-niners"? In *A Nephew from America*, an unattached ladies' man suddenly discovers that his late brother had a son in America, who is now an adult. And his new nephew is in love, and needs his uncle's assistance. Will true love, and kinship, win out?

Accompanying the two plays is an afterword on Verne's 1867 trip to the United States, and its lasting inspiration; some one-third of the author's stories would include American characters, settings, or themes.

The book is profusely illustrated with original engravings from Verne's time. Translation is by Kieran O'Driscoll, a leading expert on Verne in the English language, who is also translator of other Verne short stories and novels, and author of a study of more than a century of different translations of Verne's *Around the World in Eighty Days*.

Worlds Known and Unknown

Jules Verne's fabled tales of science fiction and adventure, the "Extraordinary Journeys," were subtitled "Worlds Known and Unknown." Hence, this is an appropriate title itself for the final volume of the Palik series. *Worlds Known and Unknown* is an anthology featuring a wide variety of the author's most astonishing shorter works, and with each is critical commentary and illustrations chosen from the original engravings that accompanied the first French publications of Verne. In these pages, the reader will experience such treats as Verne's own account of his youth, his first chronicles of ballooning, and how he imagined a love story between Leonardo da Vinci and Mona Lisa.

In 2003, the North American Jules Verne Society also co-published (with Prometheus) the Verne play, **Journey through the Impossible**. A tale of fantasy and science fiction, *Journey through the Impossible* ran for 97 performances in Paris in 1882 and 1883. In three acts, the characters go first to the center of the Earth, then under the sea, and finally into outer space to the imaginary extrasolar planet Altor. Characters from *Journey to the Center of the Earth, From the Earth to the Moon, Twenty Thousand Leagues under the Sea*, and *A Fancy of Doctor Ox* appear again in *Journey through the Impossible*. The players include Captain Nemo, the lunar travelers Barbicane and Michel Ardan, Doctor Ox, and Professor Lidenbrock, after his trip to the center of the earth. Translation of *Journey through the Impossible* is by Edward Baxter, with introduction and notes by Jean-Michel Margot, along with reviews from the play's first presentation. Roger Leyonmark provides new illustrations in the style of the 19th century woodcuts that first illustrated French editions of Verne works, and the original engravings from the play are also featured. This is both the first complete edition in any language and the first English translation of a surprising work, by the popular Frenchman whose writing continue to delight readers—and audiences—to this day.

For additional details, reviews, and links to order the books, see the North American Jules Verne Society's website, najvs.org.

The North American Jules Verne Society

JULES VERNE WAS A FRENCHMAN, born in Nantes in 1828, who lived most of his life in Amiens, where he passed away in 1905. Despite his nationality, Verne has always had an exceptional popularity among English-language readers, one which the North American Jules Verne Society celebrates today as the successor to previous organizations.

The first group of Verne enthusiasts was formed, not in Verne's own France, but in England. The Jules Verne Confederacy began in 1921 at Dartmouth Royal Naval College, publishing *Nautilus*, a literary magazine in tribute to Verne and his son Michel, with whom they were in regular contact until Michel's death in 1925. The most permanent legacy of the Confederacy came with the publication of the Everyman's Library edition of *Five Weeks in a Balloon and Around the World in Eighty Days* in 1926, reprinted as late as 1966. Not only did it contain some of the first new, corrected translations, but the introduction by members of the Confederacy offered one of the earliest thoughtful critical overviews and bibliographies of Verne.

In France, the Société Jules Verne was formed in 1935, but their work would be interrupted by war and did not resume until 1967. Meanwhile, the American Jules Verne Society began a 20-year association. It was initiated when Willis E. Hurd penned an article, "A Collector and His Jules Verne," for the August 1936 issue of *Hobbies*, recounting his discovery that most of Verne's novels available in English had received many different translations, under widely divergent titles. A number of enthusiasts read Hurd's pioneering analysis, and a network formed. Hurd's retirement allowed him to take an interest in authoring English versions of some of Verne's untranslated stories. His collection would be willed to the Library of Congress and the volumes of another American Jules Verne Society member, James C. Iraldi, were deposited at Indiana University's Lilly Library. Iraldi was still active in the late 1960s when Ron Miller and Laurence Knight began the Dakkar Grotto, publishing two issues of a journal entitled *Dakkar*, after Captain Nemo's original Indian name.

In 1993, the North American Jules Verne Society (NAJVS) formed, and has steadily grown with annual meetings and a peer-reviewed newsletter, *Extraordinary Voyages*. Although founded largely by collectors, the group now includes scholars and readers generally, to span all types of Verne admirers. In 2003, NAJVS undertook its first book publication, Verne's science fiction play, *Journey through the Impossible*, with the Palik series of first-time translations commencing seven years later.

The Society is a not-for-profit corporation with these goals and objectives:

- To promote interest in Jules Verne and his writings.
- To provide a forum for the interchange of information and materials about and/or relating to Jules Verne and his works, such as annual meetings with workshops and presentations.
- To stimulate Jules Verne research.
- To publish a newsletter, *Extraordinary Voyages*, with articles about Jules Verne and Society related issues.

Information on membership and activities, along with various educational activities, may be found at the society's website, najvs.org, as well as on Facebook.

www.ingramcontent.com/pod-product-compliance
Lightning Source LLC
Chambersburg PA
CBHW070532170426
43200CB00011B/2398